Systemic Competitiveness:
New Governance Patterns for Industrial Development

SYSTEMIC COMPETITIVENESS

New Governance Patterns for Industrial Development

KLAUS ESSER
WOLFGANG HILLEBRAND
DIRK MESSNER
JÖRG MEYER-STAMER

Routledge
Taylor & Francis Group
New York   London

First published in 1996 by
FRANK CASS & CO. LTD.

This edition published 2013 by Routledge

711 Third Avenue, New York, NY 10017
2 Park Square, Milton Park, Abingdon, Oxon 0X14 4RN

Routledge is an imprint of the Taylor & Francis Group, an informa business

Copyright © 1996 GDI/Frank Cass

British Library Cataloguing in Publication Data
A catalogue record for this book is available from the British Library.

ISBN 978-0-714-64251-2

Library of Congress Cataloging-in-Publication Data
A catalogue record for this book is available from the Library of Congress.

Contents

Boxes, Figures, and Tables in the Text

Abbreviations

ASEAN	Association of South East Asian Nations
CACM	Central American Common Market
CAD	Computer aided design
CAM	Computer aided manufacturing
CAP	Computer aided planning
CAQ	Computer aided quality control
CARICOM	Caribbean Community Market
CNC	Computer- numerically controlled machine
COMECON	Council for Mutual Economic Assistance
CU	Currency union
DC	Developing country
EC	European Community
EEC	European Economic Community
ESID	Ecologically sustainable industrial development
FTZ	Free-trade zone
GDP	Gross domestic product
IC	Industrialized country
IMF	International Monetary Fund
LDC	Least developed country
MERCOSUR	Mercado Común del Sur (Argentina, Brazil, Paraguay, Uruguay
MITI	Ministry of Trade and Industry (Japan)
MSTQ	Measuring, standards, testing, and quality assurance
NAFTA	North American Free Trade Area
NTB	Non-tariff trade barrier
NIC	Newly industrializing country
ODM	Original design manufacturing
OECD	Organisation for Economic Cooperation and Development
OEM	Original equipment manufacturing
PPS	Production planning and control system
R&D	Research and development
SME	Small and medium-sized enterprises
TC	Trading company

| UNIDO | United Nations Industrial Development Organization |
| WTO | World Trade Organization |

Introduction and Summary[1]

Following the failure of one-sidedly inward-looking and interventionist industrialization concepts in the South and in the socialist planned economies, nearly all countries sought orientation in the concept of market economy (Esser 1993, Mármora and Messner 1992). Analyses of the experiences made in OECD countries and a group of especially competitive East and Southeast Asian countries have shown that patterns of market economy and governance can differ considerably. The most competitive countries are those that do not put all their bets on competition between isolated firms, unconditioned free trade, and the state as an institution of regulation and supervision. Rather, the most successful countries are those that actively shape locational and competitive advantages (Hillebrand 1995). In a global economic environment marked by new patterns of competition, organizational concepts, and technologies, the most efficient countries turn out to be those in which groups of relevant actors succeed in organizing rapid and effective learning and decision-making processes and shaping the business environment in accordance with the new requirements that are emerging:

- The new pattern of competition is marked by knowledge- and technology-based competitive advantages; competitive advantages based on inherited factor endowments are losing their significance.

- Firms are experiencing the emergence of new organizational structures characterized by less hierarchic organizational concepts (team work, decentralization of decision-making processes, split-ups of large enterprises to form strategic business units). The firms are embedded in dense technological and productive networks (industrial clusters, industrial districts, business alliances, long-term contractual arrangements with suppliers).

- Radical technical change gives rise both to a restructuring of old industries and a creation of new ones and to substitution processes that see traditional raw materials being edged out by new ones (e.g. copper by glass fiber, steel and aluminium by new materials).

–   In the political sphere, the new pattern of competition requires active policies aimed at shaping industrial locations. Their formulation and implementation is based on cooperative approaches that focus the know-how provided by firms, science, and the public sector (policy networks), in this way complementing the market mechanism.

Essentially, the competitiveness of firms is based on a societal arrangement in which the interplay of competition-relevant factors, actors, and policies at different levels plus a frame of reference in which these levels can interact lead to competitive advantages. The term used by the OECD (1992, 243) to describe the competitiveness that emerges in this way is "structural". We prefer the term "systemic competitiveness" to emphasize that an economy's competitiveness rests on purposive and intermeshed measures at four system levels (the meta-, macro-, meso-, and microlevels) and a multidimensional guidance concept consisting of competition, dialogue, and shared decision-making and integrating the most important groups of actors.

Three elements are important at the **metalevel**: first, a social consensus on the guiding principle of market and world-market orientation; second, a basic pattern of legal, political, economic, and overall social organization that permits the strengths of the relevant actors to be focused, sets in motion social communication and learning processes, and bolsters national innovative, competitive and growth advantages; and third, the willingness and ability to implement a medium- to long-term strategy of competition-oriented techno-industrial development. Competitive strength calls for high levels of ability in organization, interaction, and strategy on the part of groups of national actors, who, in the end, will have to strive to realize a systems management encompassing all of society.

The main concern at the **macrolevel** is to create the framework for effective competition to ensure that pressure is brought to bear on firms to increase their productivity, reducing the gap with the firms most innovative and competitive at the international level. The *sine qua non* for this is: a stable macroeconomic framework that ensures undistorted prices and favorable financing terms; a competition policy that prevents the emergence of monopoly situations; an exchange-rate and trade policy that does not obstruct exports, while at the same time avoiding adjustment processes that overtax the response potential of even adaptable firms and shunning ruinous import competition that can lead to high trade deficits.

The key issue at the **microlevel** is an effective management of technical and organizational learning processes at the firm level, effective technology management being the necessary condition of continuous product and process innovation. Moreover, management of this sort must be geared to optimizing the inter-firm division of labor by encouraging close interaction between industrial firms, suppliers, service firms, and specialized R&D institutions and to intensifying producer-user contacts.

The **mesolevel** is concerned with shaping the specific environment in which firms operate. This is where the state and societal actors on the national, regional, and local level are creating locational advantages. Of particular significance are: a competition-related configuration of material infrastructure (transportation, communications, and energy systems) and sectoral policies, above all education/training policy, research policy, and technology policy; a specifically formulated trade policy and regulatory systems (e.g. environmental standards, technical safety standards) that contribute to the emergence of specific national competitive advantages. An import protection policy for emerging industries with a lot of development potential – limited in time and tied to clear-cut performance criteria – can facilitate the process of building competitive advantages at firm level. Within individual countries, policy formulation and implementation on the regional and local level have gained in significance. Regional or local administrations, R&D institutions, and local business groups can interact closely to enhance the quality of an industrial location. How important the mesolevel is becomes evident in developing countries (DCs) in which an expected economic reactivation has failed to materialize, even though stable macroeconomic framework conditions have been created there, because production locations are underdeveloped and, in particular, the mesolevel has been neglected.

Like the case of the microlevel, the mesolevel also requires development of new patterns of organization and guidance. The traditional pattern of government control (top-down decision-making processes, lobbying activities aimed at pushing through particularist interests in the formulation of policy) is complemented by new patterns of governance (Messner 1995). The necessary resources for shaping locational advantages and guidance activities (money, know-how, ideas) are widely dispersed across both public and private actors. Therefore, it is desirable that organizational patterns emerge that are characterized by mutual information, inclusion of special interests, and joint problem-solving mechanisms, and these form the basis of decision-making processes. The new governance pattern is crucial once government programs have often been relatively ineffective because the firms concerned were not involved in the policy formulation, and the programs were thus misguided (e.g. vocational training, R&D). The state here acts as an impulse generator or moderator between firms and the associations representing them, between science and intermediary institutions. It uses dialogue as a means of detecting weak points, exploring scopes of action, and working out medium-term visions that can serve as guidelines for government mesopolicies and private initiative alike.

The shaping of industrial locations becomes a continuous process based on the autonomous efforts of firms, science, and the state, and the concerted action of private and public actors. The shaping of structures at the mesolevel therefore requires, aside from high levels of technocratic competence on the part of government actors, a high degree of social-organizational ability and the willingness of the relevant groups of actors to engage in decision-making mechanisms based on strategic interaction and keyed to solving problems through cooperative effort.

Regional cooperation and integration on the supra-national level and the international arena are also gaining significance for efforts aimed at creating national competitive and locational advantages (Esser 1994):

- Cooperation between neighboring states in regional trade and integration groups is becoming increasingly more important as a means of enlarging markets, thus stimulating the interest of domestic and foreign investors, and jointly improving the supply conditions faced by the economies concerned, e.g. regional transportation, telecommunications and energy networks or the technology base.

- Following the collapse of the socialist states and the failure of state-capitalist development strategies out of touch with the world market, a world economy has, for the first time, begun to emerge in the 1990s which includes all nations. A globalized economy calls for international regulations devised to ensure a minimum of control and guidance of global market processes. Priority considerations here include agreements on further reductions of trade impediments, in particular of protectionist barriers erected by industrialized countries (ICs) against products from developing countries, and regulation of the international financial markets.

The concept of "systemic competitiveness" should be understood as a frame of reference for industrialized and developing countries alike, one aimed at developing competitive advantages inside nation states. The crucial point is that the medium- to long-term vision and the interaction between the actors are geared to optimizing performance potentials at the different system levels and mobilizing the creativity potentials of various social actors. The present study develops lines of orientation in four steps:

Part I sketches points of departure for reflections on systemic competitiveness. Enterprises and states are faced with great new demands in view of the techno-economic-social paradigm that is emerging. The determinants of international competitiveness are changing at all four system levels. The potential of different country groups to anticipate and respond to the new demands differs considerably.

Part II discusses the individual determinants of systemic competitiveness at the four system levels: the metalevel determines the extent to which societies are in a position to develop adequate national control and guidance capacities. The macrolevel serves in particular to ensure and safeguard the existence of stable macroeconomic framework conditions. It is at the microlevel that new best practices of production, firm-level R&D, and inter-firm interaction take shape. At the mesolevel, innovative forms of interaction between firms, government, and intermediary institutions, reflected in dialogue and networking, and reforms of sectoral policies (training and advanced training, research and technology, finance, trade and environmental policies) gain their significance.

Part III describes the process of developing systemic competitiveness in industrially backward countries. The countries in the transitional phase from an inward-looking strategy to one oriented toward the world market face especially great problems. The firms in these countries must rapidly learn to eliminate shortcomings in all functional areas, i.e. to optimize their production processes, engage in product development, enter into active marketing (market research, market cultivation), and create networked structures with other firms. A key ingredient in a successful turn-around is the ability of the central groups of actors to set priorities and define sequences. It is important to develop as early as possible close interaction between government and strategic groups and to set a strategic dialogue in motion. An important feature here is to gradually ensure national control over the industrialization process and to assess correctly domestic industry's potential for adjustment and restructuring. In view of the increasing significance of regional trade groups in the North, it is also essential to develop efforts aimed at integrating developing countries into such groups or to accelerate the progress of regional cooperation and mutual integration.

Part IV, an excursus, contextualizes competitive orientation, social justice, and the sustainability of development. The emergence of systemic competitiveness by no means leads automatically to a broad improvement of living conditions and ecologically sustainable development. The forms of guidance and control that prove necessary with regard to the development of systemic competitiveness can, however, also be used to develop the relations between labor and capital, production and distribution, and economics and ecology in keeping with specific economic and social needs. The pattern of organization and control presented here is sufficiently open to allow integration of the dimensions of competitiveness, distribution, and ecology.

Part I International Competitiveness – New Requirements

1 Points of Departure for Reflections on International Competitiveness

1.1 Dynamics of Technological Change, Industrial Development, and the World Economy

1. Industrial change is a highly dynamic process. Radical technical and organizational change is affecting all countries, everywhere requiring processes of adjustment. New technologies have led to a spatial expansion of the process of industrialization; this is today a worldwide phenomenon. Individual nation states, to say nothing of industrially underdeveloped countries, are unable to influence any more than a limited number of the factors that shape the dynamism of science and technology and the specific scientific-technological regimes resulting from it.

In the course of the industrial development of today's advanced countries, the organizational pattern of industry and society alike has undergone a number of sweeping changes (Freeman 1987, 68-75). Basic inventions and discoveries set off waves of innovation that lead to a reexamination of important elements of existing patterns, in particular as established technologies and organizational patterns require ever larger efforts for ever smaller improvements. A transitional phase will see a new organizational pattern gaining a foothold in more and more areas of economy and society. The shape this takes on varies from country to country, depending on specific national conditions, making it possible to distinguish between specific national development profiles, say in Denmark or Japan. Developing countries, too, form specific profiles in the course of their industrial development. This is true of national patterns of market economy no less than it is for national competitive advantages (Porter 1990). No specific profile can easily be copied; but societies can use other countries' experiences to stimulate and enrich their learning processes.

Even following a transitional phase, i.e. in phases in which an organizational pattern is relatively stable, technological and organizational change continues; this takes the shape, for instance, of incremental product and process innovations, more refined market-entry concepts, improved managerial techniques, and changing patterns of industrial relations. The reasons why, at firm level and at government level, elements of the existing organizational pattern are constantly modified, or indeed replaced, may include sharper cost competition, a crisis of the welfare state, or mounting environmental problems. Even a gradual change of organizational patterns will stamp specifically a country's market economy and shape its specialization patterns vis-à-vis the world economy.

2. The trends toward globalization, long since visible in science, technological change, industrialization processes, and the operations of major firms, have substantially intensified in recent years. Every dynamic industrialization process on the national level has at the same time a global dimension, since such processes affect the position of all countries integrated into world trade and are themselves influenced by the expansive forces radiating from the industries of competing countries.

Any sustainably dynamic or, indeed, late industrialization process must take shape inside the boundaries marked by the rough pattern of world-market-oriented industrial development emerging in the most innovative and competitive industrialized countries. There is no path outside the frame of reference defined by the "world market". The experience of one-sidedly inward-looking socialist and state-capitalist countries is instructive here: The technical-organizational-social learning processes of firms, the state, and intermediary organizations were slow to develop in such countries (Esser 1993). They tended to neglect the development of competition-oriented structures. Fueled by incentive structures aimed against agriculture and exports, what instead emerged was an isolated industrial sector, and its development was largely determined by government targets, state intervention, and domestic demand. Compared with the advances in productivity achieved by market- and world-market-oriented economies, these countries' productivity performance was weak. The approaches to industrialization proceeding along these lines collapsed toward the end of the 1980s.

3. As the worldwide confrontation in ideology and power between Western and Eastern industrialized countries declined in significance, the political-military bipolarity marking the postwar era approached its end. This bipolarity is in the process of being superseded – for the foreseeable future – by a new tripolar constellation made of the economically strongest groups of countries in North America, Western Europe, and East Asia. The techno-industrial race between these three groups is intensifying. What has been termed the "primacy of economics" (including market economy, science, and technology; Bergsten 1992) is clearly gaining worldwide ascendancy here. The former constraints to join one political-military-ideological camp or the other are being replaced by new economic and policy mechanisms (e.g. the concept of structural adjustment) geared, throughout the world, to a strengthening of market forces, specialization with an eye to the world market, and heightened integration into the international financial system.

4. Although today nearly all countries are geared to the concept of market economy, seeking closer integration into the world economy, the specific patterns of free-enterprise organization and control differ quite substantially, as is shown by analyses of the individual experiences of OECD countries and the group of especially competitive East Asian and Southeast Asian countries (OTA 1991; Nelson 1993; OECD 1993; OECD 1994; Hollingsworth and Streeck 1994).

The demands made by the process of technological change and world-market-oriented competition have proven very high for the countries that have until now have been inward-oriented. What is important in the transitional phase is that such countries succeed in implementing a critical mass of market-oriented reforms that will make their reorientation irreversible. Yet it is precisely this phase that is accompanied by difficult problems: market theory is often understood, and implemented, in an abbreviated form, and this leads to a situation in which economic, social, and ecological imbalances are exacerbated (Klitgaard 1991, Amsden, Kochanowicz and Taylor 1994). The fact is often ignored that scopes for industrialization, competition, and welfare first have to be created by recognizing and deliberately exploiting latent development potentials with an eye to the frame of reference defined by the world economy.

It is crucial for societies in the transitional phase between domestic and world market orientation to ask themselves, at the earliest possible point of time, how they wish to develop their future free-market organizational pattern. If they neglect this issue so central to coming to terms with the process of techno-industrial structural change, they are likely to meet with failure in view of the low levels of competitiveness of their economies – especially under conditions of rapid import liberalization and burgeoning import competition. The consequence is that market-oriented reforms are discredited, adjustment costs are unnecessarily high, and the positive effects on growth and employment are slow to materialize. Only if they succeed in developing sufficiently effective organizational patterns will such countries have a chance of meeting the heightened economic, social, and ecological demands facing them.

5. All countries are faced here with an onerous challenge: the drive for innovation and invention that is today emerging is not restricted to a limited number of key technologies. It is instead leading to far-reaching change in a large number of mutually reinforcing technological fields which may in part overlap. The new push may invalidate an existing organizational pattern, for instance a Taylorist-Fordist organization of factory production. It will lead to an intensive process

of searching and adapting, a process further fostered by the great pressure exerted by global competition for quality locations and growth. In all, a new technical-economic-social paradigm is taking shape,[2] i.e. a new organizational pattern in industry and society alike.

To cope with new challenges and new search processes, societies need a pronounced political will to marshal forces, to experiment with elements of a newly emerging organizational pattern, and in the end to combine them in a creative way. The first concern is to relax, or even to break up, institutionally hardened lines between state, industry, and civil society so as to improve the legal-institutional, sociostructural, infrastructural, and process- and regime-related conditions in favor of market economy and a heightened international competitiveness. When and to what extent a fully differentiated and effective new organizational pattern will emerge that will make it possible to shape new economic, political-administrative, and social structures is contingent upon the degree to which the important groups of actors are able to become autonomous, articulate their own interests, and interact cooperatively. To be sure, the new pattern must remain flexible enough to be modified when new demands emerge. In view of the current process of technological change, the broad-based competitive strategies of numerous OECD countries and NICs, and the – on the whole – growing number of competitors in the world market, it will prove particularly difficult for the industrially underdeveloped countries to develop world-market competence.

1.2   National Transformation Capacity: Processes of Adjustment, Decline, and Advance

National transformation capacity is determined by a country's ability to come to grips with the demands posed by technological change, the world economy, national social groups, and the permanent character of the development process. The competence required to safeguard and heighten national transformation capacity differs considerably from country to country and in the course of development taken by every individual country. One condition essential to the success of developing countries is an orientation in terms of the market and the world market. Further conditions are: national and social integration, a moderate rate of population growth, the political will to devise and implement a realistic strategy, an organizational pattern and control concept that foster creativity and safeguard an innovative dynamic and a competitive orientation, and, in addition, the willingness to place one's own learning processes in the broader context constituted by the learning processes of other successful countries.

Over the course of time, national transformation capacity is open to considerable fluctuation. If this capacity declines in one country at the same time that it is undergoing dynamic development in other countries, the positions in the international hierarchy may change considerably. Such redefinitions are – seen in terms of several decades – not at all seldom. Processes of decline faced by countries due to a lack of adaptability are matched by processes of technological and industrial progress in other countries.

1. The technical-organizational potential of the highly innovative and competitive pioneering countries, at the same time the sites of the most important pioneering firms, is as a rule sufficient to induce them to supplement their own basic inventions and discoveries by taking over know-how and to create the conditions required to adapt their economies to altered conditions in the world economy. Furthermore, the framework provided by competition between industrialized countries for industrial locations and economic growth fosters a process involving an exchange of mutually beneficial learning elements. State, economy, and science join forces to advance transfers of know-how. It is the strong industrialized countries that are taking the lead in shaping many of the features of their regional economies and the world economy alike.

Yet even industrialized countries experience, again and again, great pressure to adjust, and this in turn engenders resistance and impediments. The pressure arises when such countries pursue, over a longer period of time, one-sidedly market- or state-oriented policies and when economic, social, and political structures have been allowed to rigidify.

Adjustment crises are often difficult to overcome, even when high levels of innovativeness are sustained. This tends to be the case whenever a phase of high economic growth has given rise to a marked disparity between public social services and the innovative and competitive power of the economy concerned.

The relationship between business firms and nation states entails one particularly difficult problem. A growing number of large corporations from the industrialized countries have broken free of their one-sided dependence on a single national base and are now turning to account the national competitive advantages offered by different countries; some corporations are "globalizing", although strategic corporate management and a significant percentage of R&D more often than not remain in the home country (Brainard 1993). At the same time the new requirements posed by technology and the world market make it clear that the innovative and competitive power of firms is not at all determined solely by the firms themselves, one major factor being the transformation capacity of their national base. Countries in which the competence and interaction of the most important groups of actors is sufficient to create appropriate technical-organizational-social conditions have a significant national competitive advantage. As a rule, and despite the trend toward globalization, the private-sector actors are for the most part national or behave in the sense of national corporations; but in some countries (like Singapore) the national competitive advantage is enjoyed by firms that are largely foreign-owned.

The market and world-market orientation now shared by nearly all countries gives rise to another problem. Competitiveness is on the rise in a growing number of countries. This is true for traditional, labor-intensive, resource-based, and technology-intensive industrial goods. Many countries offer locational advantages that induce firms from industrialized countries to intensify their commitment there. With an eye to important markets, the governments of industrialized countries have begun to support selectively the exports and investment activity in which their firms are engaged. The adjustment problems stemming from "global integration," e.g. in the field of employment, are growing quickly, and these problems call for solutions that go beyond any national frame of reference. Approaches keyed to stepped-up regional cooperation and integration between the industrialized countries are being expanded, and similar approaches are being developed in the South.

2. Many countries in the midst of industrialization processes are – not unlike the case of today's industrialized countries in earlier phases – succeeding in setting in motion dynamic learning processes. They aim at adjusting rapidly to the demands posed by the currently emerging technical-organizational-social paradigm, and they try to strengthen domestic firms and national competitive advantages. If the specific national, regional, and global conditions involved in shaping a country's profile and path to growth do not obstruct efforts of this kind, if, in addition, there is a strong political will to impart to society a direction of this sort, and if an effective pattern of organization, control, and strategy is developed, this can give rise to a process of rapid innovative imitation that may even extend to autonomous innovation and processes of latecomer industrialization (Hillebrand 1991). Such processes involving a dynamic mobilization of national development potentials are emerging in particular in East and Southeast Asia – including China – and are leading to a situation in which, even in technology-intensive industries, established competitive positions of industrialized countries are being challenged.

3. Even hierarchies of firms are subject to a constant process of change. In phases of relative technical-organizational stability, leading firms can erect barriers to entry which, on the one hand, are conducive to their growth and allow them to reap above-average returns and which, on the other hand, make it possible for them to realize econo-mies of scale and to engage in major R&D efforts. But in phases of radical technical-organizational change windows of opportunity open up in that established firms are frequently confronted with major problems in adapting to new technical and/or organizational require-ments; Europe's wristwatch-making industry and typewriter industry or the computer mainframe industries of the US and Japan are examples of the fatal consequences that can emerge from inadequate efforts to adapt to new organizational requirements; the European and

US automobile industries are good examples of what can happen when industries are slow to adapt to new technological requirements. Such phases open up for newcomers scopes of action that allow them to redefine the functional logic of markets and the intra-firm and inter-firm organizational pattern associated with it and/or to give (large) established firms a run for their money (Perez and Soete 1988); the success of Taiwan's microcomputer industry is a good example of this.

But most firms, in particular firms in developing countries, are forced to set their sights on holding their own in the market as early followers. The early follower starts out with existing products and proven production technologies, adapting them to national and regional conditions. Compared with the pioneering firms, early followers are faced with stiffer price competition, though they are – especially in developing countries – able to exploit systematically a great variety of cost advantages (purchase of tried-and-tested capital goods, taking advantage of stiff supplier competition; getting along without automation of individual subfunctions; use of favorably priced standard components; less R&D personnel; wage-cost advantages at all functional levels; cost-effective use of infrastructure; etc.). Early followers are, however, also faced with the challenge of having constantly to improve their products, production techniques, and organizational concepts and to identify in time, and respond to, technological discontinuities and fundamentally new demand conditions. If they are unsuccessful, early followers will go under in competition. If, however, such firms purposively strengthen existing potentials and develop an ambitious long-term business strategy, the road may be open for them to join the group of pioneers. The demands placed by imitative competition on firms and the quality of their locations are, on the whole, high.

2   Development of World-Market Competence – Competing Guiding Principles

The – empirically and conceptually – well-founded discussion on strategies and approaches suitable to develop internationally competitive industries, a discussion that has gained in depth and breadth especially since the end of the 1980s, differs fundamentally from the positions represented by followers of the neoliberal or neoclassical schools of thought. On the basis of the latter schools of thought, or theoretical edifices, specific – yet similar – economic-policy concepts have, since the end of the 1970s, been devised to safeguard the dynamism and international competitiveness of industrialized and developing countries alike:

–   At OECD level, the concept of positive adjustment was developed at the end of the 1970s as a guiding principle of economic policy, an approach intended as a basic concept keyed to formulating optimal framework conditions for the process of structural economic adjustment (OECD 1979).

–   The discussion on a structural adjustment policy appropriate for developing countries, which has occupied World Bank and International Monetary Fund (IMF) since the end of the 1970s, displays distinct parallels to the OECD's concept of "positive adjustment". Developing countries, too, are expected by World Bank and IMF to gear their policy-thinking to the concept of competitive economy, i.e. competition at home and free trade abroad, the recipe they claim to have been followed by the especially successful first- and second-generation export-oriented NICs in East and Southeast Asia.

Developing countries that wish to build up internationally competitive industries on the basis of conscious choices of strategies and policies are therefore faced with difficult basic decisions as regards economic policy and *Ordnungspolitik* (i.e. the regulatory-policy that defines the general framework, incentives, and property rights). The question is whether to seek orientation in terms of the neoliberal concept of international competitiveness or the concept of *structural* or *systemic competitiveness*.

2.1   Neoliberal Recommendations and Competing Views

Proponents of neoliberal economic concepts proceed on the assumption

> "... that a competition-oriented market economy is the best mechanism to come to grips, constructively, flexibly, and without incurring undue costs, with the challenges presented by constantly changing social, economic, and technical environmental conditions... One further condition important to the functioning of the free-enterprise system is the existence of a more or less stable international framework and the confidence of market participants in the continuity of a free system of multilateral trade and payments..." (Michalski 1985, 217 f.).

The best option for coming to terms with the process structural industrial change is seen above all in a preventive policy

> "in which governments rely primarily on the ability of a market economy to regulate itself and to coordinate decentrally formulated producer and consumer decisions. In this case the priority of economic activity is concentrated in *Ordnungspolitik* and competition policy and rests on macroeconomic measures involved in monetary, fiscal, and credit policy. With regard to structural adjustment, important conditions for the success of any such policy include mobility of labor and capital, currency stability at flexible relative prices, support for private initiative, and the ability of market participants to respond positively to changing conditions in their social, economic, and technological environment." (ibid., 224 f.)

It follows from the complementary neoclassical doctrine of comparative cost advantages that a country is competitive when it specializes in the production and export of the goods according to its factor endowment. According to Balassa's stages approach to comparative advantage, DCs have a comparative advantage in the production of standardized labor-intensive goods. Somewhat more advanced countries lose their competitive advantages in the area of simple labor-intensive products, and do best to look more to standardized capital-intensive product lines. Countries that have reached a higher level of development would be best advised to initiate a restructuring process leading away from capital-intensive industries and in the direction of skill- and research-intensive industries (Balassa 1977).

Representatives of a "voluntarist" economic policy and structuralist theories of development, on the other hand, cast doubt on both the analyses attributing the rise of the first- and second-generation NICs and their export successes to their implementation of neoliberal policy concepts and on the cogency of the recommendations aimed at advancing the industrialization process in developing countries within a framework keyed to the free competition and free-trade conditions which constitute the guiding principles of neoliberalism (Lipsey and Dobson 1987; Arndt 1988; Chenery 1975; Ffrench-Davis 1988; Bitar 1988):

First, it is argued, the neoliberal market and free-trade model lacks an adequate theoretical foundation, or must be seen as unrealistic as a result of its numerous underlying heroic assumptions – perfect competition, no barriers to entering national or international markets, no dynamic returns to scale (learning advantages), no external savings, perfect information.

Second, the argument continues, there is no empirical evidence that these concepts have been successfully implemented, if an exception is made for the special case of Hong Kong. Instead, economic practice in most OECD countries and just about all successful NICs in East and Southeast Asia is far removed from subscribing to the economic creed derived from market and competition theory or the neoclassical theory of foreign trade. Although it is conceded here that, both in the OECD and in numerous developing countries, there have indeed been a great variety of approaches aimed at deregulating markets, reducing the role of the state as entrepreneur, limiting subsidies, and opening up markets to foreign competition, nearly all countries are banking more and more on an active technology policy, comprehensive promotion concepts designed to strengthen the position of small and medium-sized firms, and protectionist measures – often outside the traditional set of tariff instruments – with an eye to holding their own in the international competition for growth.

The proponents of an active industrial policy, or representatives of the structuralist school, emphasize that it requires a precise analysis of the strategies and organizational concepts actually employed by successful industrialized countries and NICs to determine what demands must be met by developing countries if they are to build up internationally competitive industries. In other words, the argument goes, the competitive frame of reference to be developed must be viewed in the light of the findings generated by empirically oriented industry and innovation research.

2.2   Competitive Strategies in an Era of Radical Technical and Organizational Change

Until the late 1970s, industrial best practice in developed countries, i.e. the combination of best practice technology and best practice organization of production, was largely associated with the Fordist/Taylorist model of industrial production. Its main features were

–   the production of largely standardized commodities to meet mass demand,

–   The use of inflexibly linked, dedicated machines (Fordist assembly line production),

–   incremental product and process innovations,

–   intra-firm organization of work on strictly hierarchical lines, with a vigorous division of labor and each worker performing only simple, repetitive tasks (Taylorism),

- a tendency for the division of labor among firms to be loosely organized, and

- the concentration of public policy on macroeconomic management so as to compensate for fluctuations in final demand (Keynesianism).

Since the late 1970s, however, it became increasingly clear that a powerful range of new manufacturing technologies and closely connected organizational innovations, both stimulated by changes in consumption patterns, would lead to fundamental changes in industrial production methods and competitive strategies. The main features of the emerging techno-economic paradigm of flexible specialization, "as a new best practice set of rules and customs for designers, engineers, entrepreneurs and managers, which differs in many important respects from the previously prevailing paradigm" (Perez 1985, 443), are

- the manufacture of differentiated goods to meet a rapidly changing demand in differentiated, highly competitive markets;

- the use of flexible manufacturing technologies, i.e. either flexible mass production technologies as found in the automobile industry or flexible small-batch production as, e.g., in machine tool production;

- rapid product innovation as the cumulative application of new key technologies such as electronics, new materials, etc. making it possible to manufacture products with new or significantly improved properties, or entirely new types of products;

- the shortening of lead times in order to benefit from early mover advantages and respond to the shortening of product cycles; this requires, among other things, a systematic scanning of technological trends, markets and competitor strategies, close cooperation between R&D personnel, production engineers and marketing specialists, and the use of CAx technologies (CAD, CAM, CAQ);

- a combination of incremental and radical process innovations based on factory and office automation technology;

–   new management concepts stressing manpower development, intensive feedback between the various functional areas and flatter hierarchies.

Moreover, in view of the complexity of the new technologies and their systemic nature, the successful firms are no longer operating in isolation in the market. Instead, they seek to become part of technological networks in which information is exchanged and rapid learning processes about the latest techniques are occurring.

How important it is to think in terms of technological networking, in particular at a time characterized by the merging of areas of technology (technology fusion) central to industrial strategies, e.g. electronics and engineering (mechatronics), chemistry and electronics (chemitronics), and chemistry and biology (biochemistry), was emphasized by Dosi (1984, 288):

> "...the rates of innovation/imitation in user industries are often dynamically linked with the technological levels of that domestic industry where the innovations come from. The opposite holds true as well: the technological levels, the size and the competitive patterns in user industries provide a more or less conducive environment for technological innovation and/or imitation in the industry which is 'upstream', i.e. the industry originating the innovations...".

Contrary to the assumption made by the theory of competition, technical progress is therefore by no means solely the outcome of processes of trial and error undertaken by firms operating in isolation in the market. It is also heavily influenced by the quality of the industrial environment, namely its industrial structures, and the technological, physical, and institutional infrastructure, which must be actively shaped on the basis of cooperative planning procedures in which the know-how of firms, the research community, and government are pooled.

Comparing the features of the "old" and the emerging "new" industrial best practice, it becomes evident that the sources and determinants of industrial strength and competitiveness have changed substantially over the last decade. At a time when the techno-economic paradigm is changing, many ICs – despite their free-market rhetoric – are obviously in no way relying on the "more competition and free trade" and the "less government" model propagated by the neoclassical school. The organizational model currently emerging in many OECD countries is characterized not only by the growing importance attached to strategic corporate planning, symbiotic, even cooperative interaction between firms, but also by an active encouragement of key industries and technologies based on a broad social dialogue embracing notably the business community, intermediary institutions, the research community, and public authorities, the last of these assuming the important role as an initiator, stimulator, and coordinator of a broad-based competitive strategy.

2.3   Radical Technological Change and Its Implications for Competitive Strategies of DCs

For DCs, the emergence of generic technologies, including advanced flexible manufacturing technologies, since the late 1970s, the attendant major changes in the organization of industrial production process at the firm and government level, and changes in consumer preferences will eventually alter the macrocontext within which they will have to pursue their industrialization strategies in the years to come. According to a recent OECD study, the introduction of factory automation and flexible manufacturing systems means nothing less than that the NICs are gradually losing their initial comparative advantage.

> "The momentum of innovation is also altering the position of some industries in the product cycle, since they are moving from obsolescence or standardization to the new product phase. As a result, the theory of international product cycles that effectively accounted for the dynamics of the OECD-NIC

relationship in the 1970s is no longer so appropriate for inter-
preting current changes". (OECD 1988, 81)

In the end, it seems that developing countries wanting to succeed in
international markets will have no choice but to adapt to the new
industrial best practice evolving in developing countries, and this
chiefly for three reasons:

1. At a time when production functions and locational requirements of
all industries are rapidly changing, low labor costs as a main source of
competitive advantages will swiftly decline in importance. DCs must
therefore prepare themselves for an increase in importance of man-
made competitive advantages that can be developed only on the basis
of state-of-the-art technologies and managerial concepts.

2. Demand for manufactures has clearly shifted toward differentiated
and higher-quality products, while the market prospects for simple,
standardized goods will be fairly limited in the future. Exports of non-
standardized goods at competitive prices will be possible, however,
only if modern (flexible) manufacturing technologies and modern
concepts of organizing production in and between firms are used.

3. In view of the complexity and the systemic nature of the new
technologies, the firms of developing countries – like their counterparts
in ICs – will also have to become part of technological networks and
seek a symbiosis between the principles of competition and cooperation. Networked firms are in a far more favorable position than firms
operating in isolation in the market in that they are better able

–   to benefit from advantages stemming from a consciously organ-
    ized division of labor among firms,

–   to tap the efficiency potential of interplay logistics,

–   to concentrate on developing specific strengths, and

–   to take advantage of the strengths of other units in the network and
    combine them with their own strengths.

Rather than establishing functionally unrelated sectors and following a strategy of "marching through the sectors" – as implied by the "stages approach to comparative advantage" – developing countries would be well advised to pursue "marching within the sectors" (Kaplinsky 1988, 22 ff), i.e. concentrate on establishing a select number of "poles of competitiveness", since a strong commitment in certain "families of industries" facilitates economizing on indirect production costs (communication costs), finer-tuned production at the several stages, more efficient quality control as well as continuous upgrading and learning within and among industries, and the timely creation of pole-related infrastructural facilities (physical, human).

It follows that under the conditions of radical technological and organizational change, government is faced with a new challenge as an actor in the process of world-market-oriented industrialization. In particular, it will not be able to eschew the role of initiator, coordinator, and stimulator. For two reasons, an active government must above all ensure that the industrialization process is based on a medium- and longer-term strategic perspective:

–   It appears rather unlikely under the conditions of radical technological and organizational change and fierce international competition, and in view of the still fragmented industrial structures in most DCs that technological networks will be able to develop here solely on the basis of a spontaneous and entirely market-regulated process. Technological networks will, rather, have to be deliberately created and supported by a set of industrial and technology policy instruments such as national subcontracting schemes, local content programs, selective import protection to encourage technological learning, specific service and R&D facilities, mission-oriented R&D schemes, etc.

–   In view of their highly limited financial, manpower, and managerial resources, developing countries cannot spread their resources thinly over the economy. They inevitably need to focus on a limited number of "poles of competitiveness" to be selected on the basis of a thorough analysis of existing industrial and technological potential, actual market trends, strategies of competing countries, and new promising areas of specialization.

An active and anticipatory structural policy initiated by an active government in no way means, however, the drafting of indicative plans by government agencies with limited knowledge. The shaping of structures must, rather, be based on national dialogue in which relevant actors participate and which thus becomes the core elements of a concept of "managed economic change".

2.4   Conclusions

Complex control and guidance systems have been developed in the Western industrialized countries and especially successful NICs with an eye to integrating, in particular, competition, cooperation, and dialogue and forming the basis for a policy involving an active shaping of structures and development of internationally competitive industries. The question is whether these systems must be interpreted as suboptimal or, conversely, can be seen as seminal organizational models. The answer given to this question necessarily depends on the theoretical frame of reference on which it is based. An active shaping of structures based on complex organizational models presents itself as a misguided approach to developing internationally competitive industries against the special background of market or competition theory. But viewed from the angle of a theory of sustainable and viable systems, that is to say, seen in the light of recent theories of guidance and control current in the social sciences (see Chapter II.1), it takes on the appearance of a basically sound and realistic concept that can be used to achieve success in coming to grips with the process of industrial and technological structural change under turbulent environmental conditions.[3]

In view of the competition among basic positions of organization theory, developing countries in the process of world-market-oriented

industrialization should no longer be obliged to subscribe to a narrow neoliberal concept, nor should attempts be made to push through the orthodox model of a neoliberal and open competitive economy by applying the lever of "fair-trade" policies and conditioning access to external funds on compliance with such policies. What will instead prove necessary is a greater openness toward more complex organizational patterns devised to develop internationally competitive industries and at the same time a differentiated discussion of different theoretical approaches and empirical experiences. Any such discussion should – and this can doubtless be said even at this stage of the game – make it clear that the alternative of "market versus plan" championed by von Hayek and others misses the point of the problems associated with the control and guidance of complex sociotechnical systems: This approach addresses only the advantages and disadvantages of control and guidance systems with a specific one-dimensional structure (Hayek 1972, 1968), thereby neglecting any consideration of the relevant alternative of "one-dimensional versus multidimensional organizational patters".

3   From Comparative Advantage to Systemic Competitiveness

3.1   The Need for Concerted Action at Four Levels

Industrial competitiveness comes about neither spontaneously via a change in the macroframework nor merely via entrepreneurship at the microlevel. It is, rather, the outcome of a pattern of complex and dynamic interaction between government, firms, intermediary institutions, and the organizational capacity of a society. One factor essential here – and to this extent we are here following the neoliberal view – is a competition-oriented incentive system that compels firms to undergo learning processes and increase their efficiency. There is, however, at the same time a need for – and here we are taking up a structuralist train of thought – selective support of firms with the aim

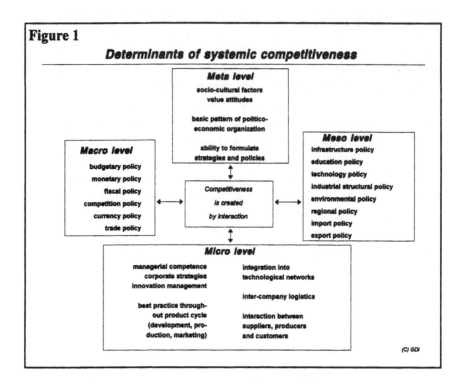

Figure 1

Determinants of systemic competitiveness

Meta level

socio-cultural factors
value attitudes

basic pattern of politico-
economic organization

ability to formulate
strategies and policies

Macro level

budgetary policy
monetary policy
fiscal policy
competition policy
currency policy
trade policy

Competitiveness
is created
by interaction

Meso level

infrastructure policy
education policy
technology policy
industrial structural policy
environmental policy
regional policy
import policy
export policy

Micro level

managerial competence
corporate strategies
innovation management

best practice through-
out product cycle
(development, pro-
duction, marketing)

integration into
technological networks

inter-company logistics

interaction between
suppliers, producers
and customers

(C) GDI

of advancing from comparative advantages to competitive advantages. The OECD (1992, 243) uses the term *structural* to designate the competitiveness which comes about in this way. The present report prefers the term systemic competitiveness as a means of stressing the following aspects. An economy's competitiveness rests both on targeted and interrelated measures at four system levels (the meta-, macro-, micro-, and mesolevels) and on a multidimensional pattern of control and guidance consisting of competition, dialogue, and joint decision-making; this pattern involves the most important groups of actors (Figure 1, Box 1).

Box 1:

The determinants of systemic competitiveness are located at four levels:

1. Metalevel

Sociocultural factors and shared values. These are, for example, essential in determining whether in a society the development of entrepreneurial dynamics are stimulated or discouraged.

The basic pattern of politico-economic organization. An outward-looking and competition-oriented (i.e. competition between firms, but also between political groups) basic pattern encourages international competitiveness, while a basic pattern geared to clientelism, protection, and inward orientation does not.

The strategy and policy competence of the social actors. International competitiveness emerges only when a society succeeds in establishing a solid consensus on this goal and developing medium-term strategies.

2. Macrolevel

Monetary policy provides for a stable framework (low inflation), without obstructing investment through excessively high interest rates.

Budgetary policy aims at achieving a manageable budget deficit with an eye to ensuring monetary stability.

Taxation policy stimulates productive investment. The graduated system of taxation is fair, transparent, and progressive.

Competition policy counters the emergence of monopolies and trusts and misuse of market power.

Currency policy is conceived in such a way as neither to obstruct exports nor to unduly raise the prices of imports.

Trade policy encourages an active integration into the world market.

3. Mesolevel

Import and export policy is managed in such a way as to protect or encourage selectively select industries for a given, limited period of time.

Infrastructure policy ensures that competitive advantages in production are not thwarted by losses in transportation and communication and that successful industries are able to find support in a modern infrastructure.

Educational policy is conceived in such a way as to ensure a broad, solid elementary education for all citizens and higher educational services for as many persons as possible; higher education is also designed with regard to needs in the fields of specialization required by the productive sector.

Box 1 (continued)

Technology policy aims above all in the direction of a broad diffusion of new technical processes and organizational concepts and in this way encourages a continuous industrial modernization process.

Regional policy aims not at a uniform distribution of industry throughout the country, but at selectively strengthening emerging industrial clusters.

The **development of new branches of industry** is initiated and stimulated by government.

Environmental policy ensures that competitiveness comes about via technical and organizational effectivity and not via exploitation of man and nature; it ensures that economic and ecological efficiency are aimed for simultaneously.

4. Microlevel

Crucial to the competitiveness of firms is **workforce qualification and managerial competence.**

Competitive firms are in a position to design and implement **strategies.**

An important condition for competitiveness is **innovation management** capacity.

The competitiveness of a firm is based on the use of **best practice along the entire value chain** (development, procurement and stock-keeping, production, marketing).

The competitiveness of firms is strengthened by **integrating them in technological networks** (with other firms and research and technology institutions).

Reorganizing **inter-firm logistics** is an important approach to increasing efficiency.

Innovative impulses result from learning processes; these processes emerge from interaction **among suppliers, producers, and customers.**

The basic pattern of "systemic competitiveness" constitutes a frame of reference for industrialized countries and developing countries alike. The medium- to long-term vision and intensive interaction between the actors should, first of all, be geared to optimizing performance potentials at the different system levels and mobilizing creativity potentials with an eye to developing competitive advantages. Moreover, a country cannot simply decide for itself which individual policies or elements of competitiveness it might pick out from the set of determinants (system levels and control and guidance instruments). Rather, particularly competitive countries present

- structures at the **metalevel** which encourage competitiveness,

- a **macroframework** that exercises performance pressure on the firms, and a structured **mesolevel** in which government and social actors come to terms on support policies and advance the formation of social structures,

- at the **microlevel** a variety of firms which at the same time aim at efficiency, quality, flexibility, and responsiveness and many of which are integrated in networks.

In contrast, most DCs are marked by severe deficits at all four levels. What approaches are available to developing countries which are in the process of establishing internationally competitive industries or intend to make existing industries competitive in the international market? Which measures must be taken first? The experiences of a number of successful and less successful countries permit the following propositions:

- It is above all important that the economic macroframework be stable (i.e. manageable inflation, budget deficit, exchange rate, and government debt; and the rules of the game not be changed constantly so that investment security is ensured) and that macropolicy emit clear, unequivocal signals that indicate to the firms that they will have to approximate to the internationally adequate level of efficiency. Trade policy can serve this end as long as protection against imports is dismantled in clearly defined stages. Competition policy can play a major role in preventing monopoly situations.

- The formulation of mesopolicies makes little sense as long as no steps have been undertaken to stabilize the macroframework. But the stabilization of the macroframework itself is merely a necessary, but not sufficient condition for the sustained development of competitiveness. Parallel to alteration of the macroframework, certain mesopolicies need to be changed (e.g. educational policy, selective import and export policy, privatization of state firms). It has, however, proven extremely difficult to provide firms mesopolicy support in an early phase of the transition process. It is frequently only possible to formulate effective mesopolicies when a development-strategic consensus is beginning to emerge (it is only here that the addressees show a willingness to enter into a dialogue) and stabilization is beginning to take effect at the macrolevel (this is the condition for substantial new investment). Technology policy, for example, will achieve its goal of strengthening the technological competence of firms only when the entrepreneurs themselves strive to attain competitiveness. Selective import protection only protects the strengthening of industries when the firms actually utilize the time to become competitive.

–   Many DCs that have long been developing with an eye to their domestic market were marked in the 1980s by social obstructions to development and a lack of consensus on the direction any future development strategy was to take (obstructions at the metalevel). Key actors must accept the new model of the world market as a frame of reference. Only then will these obstacles disappear, learning processes in economic policy thus being initiated. The more and more widespread consensus on the direction of development is a necessary condition for the establishment of policy and strategy by groups of strategic actors. This in turn is a precondition for social search processes directed toward an approximation to the new rough pattern of industrial development and the development of government and intermediary institutions which make it possible to shape the macro- and mesolevel (building consensus on politics and economic policy). The dynamics of this process will, however, differ (societal integration capacity) as a function of sociocultural structures, which change very slowly (traditions, shared values, basic social organizational and power structures).

Stabilization of the macroframework, consensus-building, and mesopolicies place great demands on society and its political-administrative system, i.e. on its organizational competence at the metalevel. Lack of ability to meet these demands is the core feature of underdevelopment. In many DCs, an incomplete process of nation-building or other unfavorable factors at the metalevel are, even over the medium term, running counter to an industrial development which aims at international competitiveness. Not many societies will run through an industrialization process so rapidly and dynamically as did the Republic of Korea or Taiwan. Nevertheless, there are in many other societies latitudes for development of the essential factors at all four levels – systemic competitiveness is not a permanent privilege of any one small group of countries.

3.2   Demands Facing Different Groups of Countries

The following four groups of countries differ considerably in their potential to anticipate and respond to the new demands posed by technology and the world market:

1. The industrialized countries have strengths at all four system levels; they are highly experienced in guidance and control. Economic exploitation of the different new technologies, the techno-industrial race among the three groups of industrialized countries (North America, Western Europe, East Asia), and the great level of competitive pressure exerted by developing countries have, however, given rise in these countries as well to a comprehensive search and adjustment process. The firms concerned are at pains to find new patterns of organization and control. The states have begun to reform the management structures of their administrations, now seen as overly costly, unimaginative, inflexible, and out of touch with their clientele (Naschold 1992, Jürgens and Naschold 1994), and optimize the complex processes involved in coordinating local, regional, national, and multilateral policy levels. Deficits in material infrastructure, in the training and R&D sectors are in the process of being uncovered. Efforts aimed at systemic coherence are underway; a key example would be a closer interlinkage of science, technology, industry, state, and intermediary organizations of civil society.

Cost-reduction strategies (deregulation, reduction of structure-conserving policies and social services, fiscal reorganization, cutting red tape) go hand in hand with a reorganization of innovation efforts. It is not only in the national context that forces are being marshaled; efforts aimed at regional cooperation and integration are also on the increase, and their goal is to further improve the supply and demand conditions under which the economy operates. This purpose is also served by coordinated government- and industry-level strategies geared to specific growth regions (e.g. Southeast Asia, Latin America). In the end, the factor crucial to the future international competitiveness of its economy is whether a country succeeds in adjusting its entire pattern of organization, control, and strategy.

2. The East and Southeast Asian countries have long had strengths at the metalevel (national coherence, consensus on the required adjustments to the basic pattern, coordinated control and guidance processes). Their high level of strategic capability is also an important factor in safeguarding stable macroeconomic framework conditions. By meeting the demands posed at the different system levels and closely interlinking these levels, they have succeeded in boosting the international competitiveness of their economies and at the same time creating the favorable social conditions required for this purpose (e.g. in the education/training sector). It is only then that an effective management of resources and energy can emerge. The locational advantages of these economies and the world-market-oriented specialization of their industry are giving rise to considerable challenges for the industrialized countries. In spite of growing competition, the latter are highly interested in direct investment in these countries and in developing close and cooperative economic ties with them. This trend will continue if the countries of East and Southeast Asia deepen their mutual techno-industrial cooperation and at the same time use, more than they have until now, social and ecological policies to bolster their organizational patterns.

3. In the more advanced countries of Central-Eastern and Eastern Europe, Latin America, and Asia, all of which went through long phases of inward orientation, the current concern is to come to successful terms with the difficult task of establishing a world-market-oriented market economy. They are as a rule faced with weaknesses at all system levels. The first important consideration is to implement a

stable macropolicy that creates economic security and generates pressure to step up productivity. As the next step, the emergence of autonomous search and learning processes in the policy fields is crucial to the development of systemic competitiveness. The concern is to trigger strong catalytic effects that bring the central elements of an already differentiated organizational pattern in line with the exigencies of a market and world-market orientation.

An important concern is to cut back the deficient points of the macroframework (e.g. in the areas of financial, fiscal, and competition policy) and to mobilize performance potentials on all system levels. Another important task is to provide selective impulses in development cooperation with the industrialized countries so as – for instance in connection with privatization – to improve inter-firm cooperation and contribute to the development of specialization profiles. To strengthen the mesolevel, it is important to counter any fragmentation of forces – a phenomenon that is often observed – by stimulating new patterns of dialogue and decision-making, thus improving the strategic capabilities of the actors concerned, and by reorganizing, or supplementing, the existing institutions in the business environment. What is meant here is above all the institutions at the interfaces between science, technology development, and production (e.g. R&D institutions, patent offices, technical universities) (Hillebrand, Messner and Meyer-Stamer 1994). Another important task is the reorganization or development of social security systems (e.g. private pension funds that also contribute to the mobilization of capital); this entails a reorientation vital to any strengthening of systemic competitiveness. Many countries in this group could, in the mid-term, turn out to be strong competitors, but also interesting partners for cooperation with the industrialized countries (Esser, Hillebrand, Messner and Meyer-Stamer 1993).

4. There are no economic alternatives to market economy on the horizon for the poor developing countries. As a rule these countries display severe weakness at all system levels. The weaknesses are for the most part especially pronounced at the metalevel: the process of nation-building is often incomplete, the level of national integration, and with it national coherence, is low, there is no robust civil society,

and the strategic capability of the relevant groups of actors is underdeveloped. Neglect of innovative, growth-related, and competitive potentials leads to symptoms of disintegration, and these are exacerbated by high levels of population growth. These problems, often accompanied by an inadequate market constitution, weak government, and firms lacking in competitive experience make it impossible for many of these countries to come to grips with the new technological and economic demands posed by the world economy. Social and political conflict potentials are accumulating in many of these countries.

This country group, too, will have to develop initiatives of its own in order to create a stable macroframework and strengthen groups of actors concerned with identifying and harnessing both their own and national performance potentials. Development of the mesolevel, often serving to create social structures and foster integration (e.g. in the education/training sector), should always be keyed to "systemic competitiveness". As a rule, the first step will entail world-market-oriented specialization in no more than one segment of economy and society. Only in this way is it possible to utilize export potentials to earn needed foreign exchange, thus initiating world-market-oriented learning processes. The first step nearly always involves exploiting resource-based advantages and wage-cost advantages. It is only on this basis that it is possible to advance into more value-added-intensive industrial sectors. Even when national forces have been brought to focus, it is often not possible, at least in the short to medium term, to come to effective terms with social problems. Here, far more than in the case of the second and third country groups, what is called for is development cooperation that at the same time contributes to ensuring survival.

Part II Sources and Determinants of Industrial Competitiveness – the Need for Concerted Action at Four Levels

1 Establishing Requirements Essential for Competitive Industries at the National Level (Metalevel)

1.1 Formation of Social Structures as a Condition of Economic Modernization

Crucial to an optimization of performance potentials at the micro-, macro-, and mesolevel are the control and governance capacity of government and forms of social organization which make it possible to mobilize the creativity potentials of various social actors. Economic modernization and the development of systemic competitiveness cannot succeed without appropriate social structures. Many DCs were until recently characterized by centralist political decision-making processes and bureaucratized, inefficient government apparatuses with a low level of governance capacity, overlaid with rentist-corporatist structures which permitted privileged groups to effectively realize their particularist interests. These power-pervaded and encrusted political structures corresponded with forms of social disintegration and fragmentation that were characterized by the exclusion of broad segments of the population as well as by political and social polarization.

The neo-liberal orthodoxy suggests economic-policy strategies which attempt to set in motion economic modernization processes by releasing market forces and reducing the scope of government. This approach often underestimates the extent to which DCs are characterized by weak markets and weak firms, an omnipresent and at the same time weak government, and weak social actors. Macroeconomic reforms initiated without establishing regulatory and governance capacities (government reform, formation of complex interlinkages between strategic actors) and formation of social structures will lend further force to the tendencies toward social disintegration. Systemic competitiveness without social integration is a futile endeavor. Building systemic competitiveness is a social transformation project that goes far beyond correcting macroeconomic framework conditions.

Social integration rests on an institutional context of action which is characterized by three features:

–   compatibility of the chief shared values, initially on the part of the strategic actors, then on the part of an expanding interlinkage of groups (minimum consensus);

–   the ability of the social actors to respond swiftly and effectively to adaptation requirements (learning and transformation capacity);

–   over the longer term, institutions, regulations and habits that make possible stable and long-term behavioral expectations (stability) and are at the same time open to new challenges (change) (Deutsch et al. 1964).

Against this background, the emergence of a basic social consensus on the direction of the changes aimed at proves to be an important element of a reorientation toward the world market. Medium-term orientations and visions are important to being able to assert future interests against current interests and generate stable expectations. If this fails, the required structural change will – as was the case in many Latin American countries in the 1980s – be deferred, thus prolonging the process of social disintegration; the bill for this is paid by weak social actors unable to articulate their interests adequately. What is needed over the medium term to overcome obstructive social structures is the development of durable patterns of social organization and an orientation of the values shared by the social actors in terms of concerted action and cooperative approaches to problem-solving.

1.2   Social Patterns of Organization and Systemic Competitiveness – the Interdependence of Meta- and Meso-level

The task involved in the process of social structural change is on the one hand to safeguard the autonomy of social institutions and organizations from encroachments on the part of government ("art of separation", Walzer 1992, 38). Cutting the bonds between the state and trade unions, industrial associations, and universities – as is occurring in many countries – will give rise to self-responsibility. Only then will such groups contribute to policy-making in a creative manner. On the other hand, government must be safeguarded from influential, privileged groups. Only a relatively autonomous government is able to orient its activities toward overall social and economic interests. It is a clear-cut separation of government, industry, and social actors, i.e. the emergence of autonomous functional subsystems, that makes it possible in the first place to develop them dynamically and innovatively. Key elements are intrinsic learning processes, flexibility and responsiveness, and dialogue and efforts to cooperatively search for all optimal solutions ("art of communication", Walzer 1992, 76) involving government and social actors.

The autonomous social actors and intermediary institutions proceed along the lines of three complementary logics. First, they optimize, on their own responsibility, their institutions or firms (inward-looking orientation); second, they represent their interests vis-à-vis government or other social actors (competition); third, they shape their own environments through cooperation and networking with public or private institutions (cooperative competition). Heightening social self-organizational competence and clustering and mobilizing and channeling creativity potentials of social actors are complementary tasks.

Government's scope in shaping the macroeconomic framework has monopoly character. The establishment of basic regulatory-policy (*Ordnungspolitik*), institutional, infrastructural conditions is indispensable to giving a direction to social and economic development and creating conditions for strengthening market forces.

Below the level of macropolicy, dynamic societies reveal an increasing measure of differentiation of organizational patterns and forms of governance. Not unlike industrial production in which new forms of organization gain ground, leading to a breakup of the Fordist paradigm, new, complex governance patterns emerge in the sphere of meso-policies aimed at selectively optimizing the economic sector and correcting the market economy with the means of social and environmental policy. Aside from the forms of governance already prevalent in societies organized along the lines of market economies – hierarchic coordination and steering in firms and public institutions, market-like coordination among firms, and hierarchic governance of society by government – network-like forms of organization are beginning to emerge, in particular at the mesolevel, which are characterized neither by simple market allocation (competition and price) nor by centralist governance mechanisms (hierarchic control and governance of interventionism exercised by government).

While market mechanisms are characterized by the absence of dedicated coordination among decentrally oriented actors and hierarchic control and governance relies on government as an autonomous governance actor, the new forms of governance are marked by loosely coupled interaction (Granovetter 1983) between private and public actors, with the goal of shaping structures in a policy field. Government here acts as an impulse generator and moderator, promoting a dialogue-oriented industrial location policy. In other words, governance mechanisms "between markets and hierarchies" (Powell 1990) are based on a coupling of the logics of free-market mechanism and hierarchic, classically statist forms of governance:

–   on the one hand, the existence and logic of action of autonomous, decentrally organized actors of the type typical for market mechanism;

–   on the other hand, the attempt typical for hierarchic governance to define medium- and long-terms goals and the instruments adequate to achieve these goals; these means are geared to shaping structures in a subsystem.

The discussion predominant in the 1980s on the topic of "market vs. government" overlooked these innovative forms involved in the shaping of social structures via a combination of market, government, and a variety of forms of self-coordination in the shadow of the market, the shadow of hierarchies, and in self-organizing networks (Scharpf 1993, Marin and Mayntz 1991).

These new forms of governance have been coined policy networks. They are the outcome of tendencies toward increasing differentiation and specialization and functional interdependencies of modernizing societies stemming from them. A policy network is an arrangement in which autonomous actors, in negotiating systems, aim at reaching joint solutions to problems. It is, in particular, a mechanism for mobilizing governance and shaping potential at the mesolevel, because it is here that the available know-how and the decision-making, program-formulation, and implementation capacities are broadly spread across a variety of private and public actors. The mesolevel can therefore be

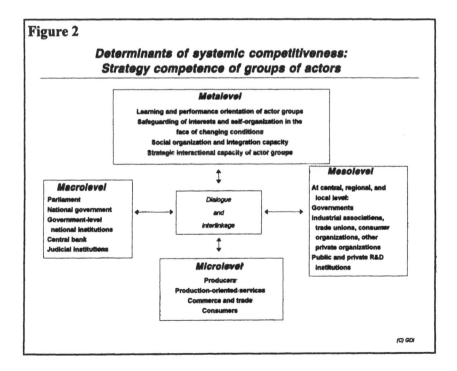

Figure 2

**Determinants of systemic competitiveness:
Strategy competence of groups of actors**

Metalevel
Learning and performance orientation of actor groups
Safeguarding of interests and self-organization in the face of changing conditions
Social organization and integration capacity
Strategic interactional capacity of actor groups

Macrolevel
Parliament
National government
Government-level national institutions
Central bank
Judicial institutions

Dialogue and interlinkage

Mesolevel
At central, regional, and local level:
Governments
Industrial associations, trade unions, consumer organizations, other private organizations
Public and private R&D institutions

Microlevel
Producers
Production-oriented services
Commerce and trade
Consumers

(C) GDI

shaped neither by government nor by the private firms or intermediary institutions on their own. What is meant here are policy arenas in which either government objectives can simply not be achieved via direct government action without cooperation from the firms and intermediary institutions (e.g. increase of competitiveness via industrial policy); an implementation of government programs by public administration would be require undue control efforts, thus rendering it too expensive (e.g. industrial safety, environmental protection regulations, technical standardization), or would prove ineffective without active cooperation of the private sector (e.g. vocational training, R&D). The shaping of structures at the mesolevel thus requires high levels of technocratic competence on the part of public actors, a high degree of social organizational skill, and a willingness on the part of the actors involved to engage in strategic interaction. Only in this way can the relative loss of autonomy of the actors, i.e. the dependence of the success of one actor (e.g. the business sector) on the effectiveness of others (e.g. public training or research institutions) [and vice versa] due to the growing differentiation of the economy, be translated into dynamic development.

Traditional forms of intervention by autonomous government are inadequate to the task of shaping the economic sector and developing specific, scarcely replicable national competitive advantages. Meso-policies are based on interactive governance patterns and interlinkage-oriented forms of organization capable of coupling the logics of hierarchic and market-like mechanisms. The network-like control forms aimed at forming structures at the mesolevel have the advantage of

- mobilizing the available know-how in a functional system, thus enhancing cooperative problem-solving capacity;

- developing joint visions and views on weaknesses, strengths, and future challenges toward which private and public institutions can seek orientation;

- increasing the legitimacy and realizability of mesopolicy;

- ensuring stability, accommodation of interests, and long-term orientation within subsystems.

1.3   Normative Patterns of Decision-Making Styles in Complex Patterns of Organization and Control

The functioning of policy networks is bound to rules, values, and action-related orientations accepted by the actors involved so as to rule out moral hazard (opportunistic advantages derived by individual actors). Important rules are:

– fair exchange,

– reciprocity,

– distribution of costs and benefits of decisions jointly taken,

– voluntary restrictions of freedom of action,

– respect for the legitimate claims associated with the interests of others (Mayntz 1991).

Actors need to accept these point as guiding principles for their actions. This is a necessary precondition for defining a common view of and a shared perspective on certain problems. A shared perspective is the precondition for problem-solving that aims at best solutions, or at least solutions that go beyond particular interests.

Stability and workability develop via density of communication, information exchange, and mutual trust. If it proves impossible to achieve an integrative and cooperative orientation of the action of the actors involved and establish fair rules of distribution governing the balance of advantages and disadvantages, networks tend toward endless disagreement, internal obstruction, and structural conservatism. Thus, societies seeking to build systemic competitiveness are largely reliant on actors capable of dealing with conflict and compromise and developing styles of decision-making geared to cooperative problem-solving (Mayntz 1991).

The term cooperative problem-solving at the mesolevel points at the experience that there are patterns of interaction beyond the conventional dichotomy of symbiotic or competitive relationships (pure coordination versus zero-sum game). Actors with both joint and conflicting interests are able to arrive at reciprocal patterns of interaction aimed at defining common goals and advancing the shaping of structures with an eye to giving a direction to economic development. The principle of reciprocity within the interlinkage presupposes egoistic motives as well as autonomous decision-making processes (e.g. improvement of the competitiveness of individual firms) and mobilizes them, while, however, at the same time channeling them in the interest of maintaining and optimizing the social system (e.g. improvements in the field of industrial siting).

These functional conditions at the mesolevel explain why authoritarian regimes, while being in a position to initiate processes of social change, are quick to reach their limits when the task at hand is to mobilize the creativity of various social actors and let them play an active role in shaping structures. The "intelligence" of democracy and interlinkage-oriented patterns of organization consists in the fact that it institutionalizes distrust in "higher" insights, solitary decisions, or any one-sidedly defined concept of public welfare and at the same time advances the incrementalist-evolutionary optimization of a path taken. Democracy constitutes the basis for mobilizing social innovation potentials as well as a barrier to artificial simplifications of problems to be solved. The alternatives hitherto sought to democratic institutions and processes and interlinkage-oriented forms of organization, i.e. hierarchic government planning in market societies on the one hand (type: Latin America) and centralistic socialism on the other hand, have proven unsuited to coming to terms with complex, networked social problem complexes. Complex, nontransparent, networked problem complexes call for complex forms of governance.

1.4   Open Interlinked Systems Capable of Learning

The close interconnection between actors, consensus orientation, and common visions are the condition of any integration and formation of social structures. However, any overly close interlocking of strategic actors and exaggerated homogenization of interests can lead to functional, cognitive, and political blockage, suffocating the creative and cumulative impulses and learning processes that emerge from the intensive interaction of autonomous actors. Without potential for conflict and corrective, subsystems interlinked too closely tend toward

- organizational myopia and ignorance vis-à-vis new development paths and necessary economic and social transition,

- externalization of costs (e.g. ecological damage) to the overall system ("subsystem paternalism", Habermas 1992, 427),

- clientelism and corruption,

- exclusion of new actors who generate new adjustment pressure, introduce new ways of looking at things, and disturb the poised equilibrium in a routinized fabric of interaction,

- rigidification, the more strongly the originally weak ties evolve into strong ties and, in the worst case, monopoly-like structures, thus eliminating the initial creativity of the form of organization situated between markets and hierarchies.

These tendencies by no means speak against interlinkage-oriented patterns of interaction on the part of the strategic social actors; instead, they speak in favor of safeguarding corrective, conflict, and opposition potential beyond the networks in the process of constitution. The more durable and successful a well-organized network proves to be in proceeding along a given development corridor, in contributing to optimization within the corridor through concerted action, the more strongly it will tend to close itself off to the outside world, to become blind to necessary changes of course that threaten the internal balance of interests and resources within the interlinkage of actors. What is required to prevent subsystem paternalism and this inherent dynamic of networked structures in the direction of incrustation is space in which to articulate "opposition potential".

Important factors are:

- the integration of conflict potential into an interlinkage of actors so as to guard against cognitive blindness (e.g. integration of trade unions and environmentalist groups to form regional conferences on the planning of industrial siting);

– the openness of the political system, which makes it possible to mobilize corrective potentials from outside existing networks.

Understood in this way, a conflict capacity on the part of the actors is an elementary component of a development strategy geared to inter-linkage and social integration.

This view of increasingly differentiated forms of social organization and governance surmounts the classical dichotomies of "market versus government" and "total autonomy of decentral actors" (liberalism) versus "totally integrated society" (socialism). Social processes of searching and learning cannot be reduced to strengthening the market plus paring down the scope of government. Rather, building systemic competitiveness is based on

– a strengthening of market forces via reduction of overregulation and creation of stable framework conditions for macropolicy;

– a disburdening of government and an increase of government efficiency by strengthening market forces and delegating control tasks to nongovernmental actors, interlinking public and private actors, strengthening subsidiary principles and social solidarity, and building sectoral networks;

– a strengthening of social self-organization capacity as the precondition for the emergence of solid social patterns of organization and complex forms of governance;

– an integration of the market into effective institutional systems, with an eye to optimizing economic development potentials and correcting destructive tendencies stemming from a market economy (social and environmental policies).

2   Macrolevel Determinants

Within a multidimensional concept of economic management which sets store on competition, cooperation, and social dialogue as a means of targeting national potentials to the development of international market competence, functioning factor and commodity markets are of key significance in safeguarding an efficient allocation of resources.

The experience made in the 1970s and 1980s has demonstrated that an unstable macroeconomic framework seriously hampers the functioning of factor and commodity markets. The most important sources of macroeconomic instability are high budget and current-account deficits:

–   Persistently high budget deficits financed by money creation inevitably lead to high inflation rates, with the consequence that the signal function of prices, and thus the functioning of the market mechanism, is largely deprived of its power.

–   Persistently high current-account deficits stemming from heavily overvalued exchange rates lead to high levels of foreign debt and a debt service that cuts sharply into national investment activity. An economy's foundations of growth are thus seriously undermined.

Any stabilization of the macroeconomic framework must therefore first and above all come to grips with the task of reforming fiscal and budgetary policy, monetary policy, and, in particular, the exchange-rate regime. Transition from an unstable to a stable macroframework is, however, apt to prove difficult for the following reasons:

–   Fighting inflation by means of a restrictive budgetary, fiscal, and monetary policy frequently leads to a curtailment not only of consumption but of investment as well, thus further cutting the economy's room for growth.

–   Macroeconomic stabilization measures are frequently able to take effect only if they are accompanied by parallel, protracted structural reforms, e.g. reform of the public economic sector, the development of an efficient financial sector, and reforms of foreign-trade policy.

–   The targets of individual reform measures often conflict, thus prolonging the time-frame needed for the reforms to take effect.

–   The adjustment costs make themselves felt directly, while the adjustment gains take some time, and is apt to entail negative developments in production, investment, and employment in the initial phase.

–   The social groups are not affected equally by the impacts of macroeconomic stabilization measures and the structural reforms accompanying them. Instead, there are in this process losers and winners and correspondingly intense domestic conflicts.

Stabilization of the macroeconomic framework thus calls for something on the order of a political tightrope act. This will succeed only if government demonstrates its resolution to push through difficult and conflict-laden reforms and manages to organize a national coalition of pro-reform forces and mobilize international support.

2.1   Safeguarding the Domestic Economic Balance

In a highly inflationary environment, the signal function of prices is neutralized. The consequence is an inefficient allocation of resources. What is crucial is therefore that government pursue a budgetary, fiscal, and monetary policy aimed at creating a stable financial environment.

1. Budgetary and fiscal policy: Reducing budget deficits at the same time requires measures on the spending and the revenue side.

–   Expenditure side: The politically more simple way to reduce government spending is to cut government investment, e.g. for education, health care, and infrastructural measures. This path, however, is a dead-end street, since it weakens the foundations for future growth. Consolidation measures must therefore start above all with consumption-related spending and the elimination of privileges for individual vested interests. This requires in particular a reduction of overemployment in the public sector, cuts in the deficits of publicly owned enterprises, cuts in military spending, and a reduction of subsidies by limiting the time for which they are granted and introducing degressive subsidy rates.

– Revenue side: Measures aimed at increasing government revenues must not be conceived merely in terms of a short-term reduction of the budget deficits; they must also take into consideration the dimensions of growth and redistribution. An approach of this sort as a rule requires a thoroughgoing restructuring of the system of taxes and levies and a strengthening of the administrative competence of the tax authorities. The tendency must be to tax consumption more than production, to focus on and tax progressively all types of income, to avoid any bias in the taxation of national and international transactions, and to take steps in the direction of introducing cost-covering fees for government services.

The package of measures required to consolidate the government budget shows that what is needed to cut budget deficits is in the end a combination of demand-side and supply-side reform measures. Thus, for instance, countries in which there is a large public economic sector will not be able to avoid restructuring and privatizing deficitary state-owned firms in order to broaden their tax base over the medium and long term.

2. Monetary policy: To stabilize the value of money, budgetary, fiscal, and monetary policy must be fine-tuned to one another. In particular, a restrictive budgetary policy ought not to be counteracted by an expansive monetary policy.

Under the conditions of an underdeveloped money and capital market, however, a stability-oriented monetary policy will be faced with narrow limits, since customary instruments like credit rationing, selective lending, and arbitrary setting of interest rates tend more to lead to further deformations in the capital and money markets rather than to prove able to influence the volume of credit to the degree desired.

An effective monetary policy in the end presupposes comprehensive reform of the financial sector. This must aim in particular at:

–   strengthening the competence of the central bank to control domestic money supply and inflows of capital from abroad,

–   developing an efficient and diversified private financial sector (banks, insurance firms),

–   safeguarding effective competition in the capital and money markets, and

–   reducing discretionary government interventions aimed at influencing credit allocation through directed credit programs.

2.2   Safeguarding the External Balance

Persistently high current account deficits restrict the scope open for growth and destabilize the economy. High current-account deficits as a rule signalize a general anti-export bias within the general economic framework and can thus be reduced only by thoroughly modifying economic policy, in particularly trade and exchange-rate policy.

Exchange-rate policy: The experience made in the 1970s and 1980s demonstrated that strongly overvalued exchange rates inevitably lead to high current-account deficits, since they above all facilitate imports and hamper the export of industrial products. Countries that accept a long-term overvaluation of their currencies impede the development of an efficient industrial production apparatus in two ways:

–   Currency-related rises in export prices lead to a situation in which the business sector no longer sees realistic chances of gearing its production to the world market as a frame of reference.

–   Artificial reduction of import prices implies that domestic firms will also lose their competitive edge in the domestic market, with the consequence that investment will tend to concentrate on non-tradable goods, or even that capital will be exported.

An exchange-rate level displaying a strong anti-export bias must therefore be avoided at all costs. What should instead be aimed at is a competitive exchange rate or a regime with a slight pro-export bias. Here too, however, the distance from a state of balance ought not to be allowed to become too great, since the prices for imported intermediate inputs and capital goods will otherwise increase excessively, wiping out the artificially low prices of domestic inputs.

The exchange rate is therefore not simply one price among others. Rather, it is the strategic variable that determines whether an economy is in a position to create the macroeconomic conditions required to establish internationally competitive industries.

Trade policy: Not unlike the case of exchange-rate policy, firms must also be given clear signals from trade policy, signals that impel them to gear their strategies to the world market as their frame of reference. A government can here choose between two clearly distinct concepts.

– General import liberalization: This approach aims at low tariffs uniform for all classes of goods. It relies on the validity of the principle of comparative cost advantages and accepts the fact that the industries that survive are in line with the factor endowment characteristic of the country. This approach is thus interested in an

   import liberalization that is at the same time non-discriminatory and swift.

– Selective import liberalization: In this case, imports are liberalized on the basis of a liberalization timetable developed in connection with an analysis of the actually foreseeable response potentials of existing industries or the development needs of new industries. Trade policy in this way becomes part and parcel of a policy of actively shaping industrial structures.

The first concept will not be able to be avoided if the control competence of government proves inadequate. The second concept aims on the one hand at not overburdening industry's adjustment capacity and on the other hand at creating time sufficient for the learning processes needed by industries. Countries such as the Republic of Korea and Taiwan have clearly opted for the second approach to import liberalization. Both countries are, indeed, good examples that the goal of progressive foreign trade liberalization as a means of increasing external pressure, and thus pressure on productivity, can be achieved without excessivley high economic and social costs.

3   Microlevel Determinants

The 1980s were, in the ICs and the advanced DCs, a phase of change at the microlevel. What emerged was a new best practice of production, intra-firm R&D, and inter-firm interaction which can be paraphrased with the terms lean production, simultaneous engineering, and just-in-time. This new best practice breaks with the conventional Taylorist-Fordist paradigm. This presents a challenge for the for the Western ICs no less pressing than it is for the DCs, because this process is rendering obsolete deeply rooted ways of seeing and acting. Approximation to the new best practice is furthermore rendered all the more complicated by the fact that the pending changes are not restricted to the firm level. They extend as well to inter-firm relations and the mesolevel.

3.1   Determinants of Competitiveness at the Firm Level

The competitiveness of firms is coming more and more to be determined at the microlevel by a firm's success or failure in simultaneously meeting four criteria.

Efficiency: The indicators are labor and capital productivity. Both must be optimized; all in all, any one-sided emphasis of merely one indicator (in the past it was labor productivity) can in the end lead to inefficiency (if, e.g., optimization of manpower utilization proceeds at the expense of warehouse stocks or high reject levels).

Quality: An indicator of growing importance in particular for DC firms – whose quality performance is often questioned by buyers in ICs – is certification as per the International Standards Organization's ISO 9000 standard system.

Flexibility: "The concept of flexibility (...) has a number of different dimensions: product flexibility (the ability to change easily to produce new products), volume flexibility (the ability to accommodate changes in volume efficiency, routing flexibility (the ability to process parts via different routes within the plant in response to breakdowns or other factors), machine flexibility (the ability to make different parts within a product family), operation flexibility (the ability to vary the sequence of operations), and process flexibility (the ability to produce a product family in different ways possibly using different materials)." (UNCTC 1990, 32)

Responsiveness: Leading firms measure this in terms of the capability to generate innovations in rapid succession (technology leadership); one indicator of innovativeness is the share of products in the overall product spectrum which has been introduced to the market within the last two to four years. Other firms see responsiveness as the ability to imitate rapidly the innovations of leading firms. One other factor is the ability to adapt swiftly to altered customer wants, changes in fashion, and the like.

In the past, management tended to see these criteria as mutually conflictive. For instance, their appeared to be a trade-off between efficiency and quality. Japanese firms have falsified this view. Thus, many firms have to give up well-established routines and organizational patterns. It will not be sufficient to selectively improve certain parts of the value chain. Rather, the value chain itself – from R&D to production to marketing and after-sales services – has to be reorganized, e.g. by eliminated barriers between firms' departments and introducing a process-oriented organizational pattern. Moreover, firms must be in a position to formulate and implement strategies; and they must above all be able to adapt these strategies at any time to modified environmental conditions.

3.2   New Organizational Concepts in Product Development

After the Second World War, more and more (major) firms began to
concentrate their R&D efforts and to separate their R&D labs from
their actual production facilities. Behind this was the expectation of
achieving in this area economies of scale (by providing technical and
administrative services used by all departments) and a reciprocal
stimulation via spontaneously evolving or deliberately organized
interdepartmental research projects.

This expectation was, however, met only in part, and the disadvantages of central, and in particular centrally financed, R&D labs have
become manifestly evident in the recent past. Some of the reasons are
that

– in connection with the spatial separation, the interactive learning
  processes between R&D and production are diminished or even
  vanish,

– the researchers and developers are without any direct contact to
  the market – i.e. to the users of the artifacts developed by them,

– the material orientation of R&D is thus no longer marked by
  problems emerging from production and impulses stemming from
  marketing, but by introspective decision-making processes.

This decoupling of R&D has led not only to a situation in which a
sizable share of development efforts ignore market needs. Even in
cases in which, in the end, the development process gives rise to a
successful product, the development itself often takes too long and
consumes an undue quantity of resources – a finding that emerges from
a comparison of Western firms with their Japanese counterparts.

Japanese auto-makers, for example, required on average just 70 % of
the time and 60 % of the engineering hours needed by their Western
competitors for product development (Womack, Jones and Roos 1990,
118). The basis of this is the organizational model of simultaneous
engineering, which includes two elements:

- At an early stage, attempts are made to involve various departments in the development process – including marketing and purchasing – and even the firm's suppliers. Internally, the link between development and other areas is intensified by transferring R&D staff over the age of forty (when they, in the Japanese view, have passed the zenith of their creativity) to other departments.

- Product development does not proceed on the cascade model, on which various departments process a project in succession; here, different activities proceed in parallel.

One further organizational innovation developed in Japan is design for manufacturing. This amounts to finding a compromise between technical product optimization and the production process instead of one-sidedly optimizing the product, thus causing high production costs, as has often been the case in Western ICs.

3.3   New Organizational Concepts in Production

The model of the 1980s for the reorganization of industrial production was the "factory of the future," in which computer-controlled machines and robots were to render man, as the source of error, superfluous. The model of the 1990s is, in contrast, "lean production" – with its close interlinkage of production and other departments, with teams of highly qualified workers in production and intensive, trust-based cooperation between suppliers and the manufacturers of end-products.

The concept of the highly automated, computer-controlled factory has failed. Corporations like General Motors that have pursued this concept have been unable to improve substantially their competitive position because there is no systematic connection between degree of automation and productivity, for "... high-tech plants that are improperly organized end up adding as many indirect technical and service workers as they remove unskilled direct workers from manual assembly tasks. What's more, they have a hard time maintaining high yield, because breakdowns in the complex machinery reduce the fraction of the total operating time that a plant is actually producing vehicles. From observing advanced robotics technology in many plants, we've devised the simple axiom that lean organization must come before high-tech process automation if a company is to gain the full benefit." (Womack, Jones and Roos 1990, 94)

Today, it is no longer the Babbage principle and Taylorization, with its benefits with regard to specialization and the safeguarding of in-plant control, that shape thinking. Rather, what appears as the chief instrument for improving efficiency, quality, flexibility, and responsiveness is the re-integration of in-plant processes and previously fragmented work processes. "Lean production", understood in this way, is, to be sure, not to be understood as an opposition between organization and technology. What is at stake is, rather, a systemic (instead of a point-for-point) approach; the issue is to scrutinize routines and supposedly "secure knowledge"; and to use reorganization to create the conditions for effective automation.

Systemic reorganization of industrial production is a three-dimensional process:

1. The first dimension is the introduction of organizational innovations:

–   new logistics concepts at the firm level, with order-related final assembly and flow optimization in manufacturing (in-plant logistics, internal just-in-time),

–   new logistics concepts at the inter-firm level, i.e. inclusion of suppliers and customers in inter-firm logistics (external just-in-time), and – associated with this – downward adjustment of vertical integration and longer-term relationships with suppliers;

–   restructuring of quality assurance, e.g. via introduction of quality circles or total quality control. "In recent years it has been proved conclusively that the old idea of having quality inspectors examine products either part-way through or at the end of the line is an extremely inefficient one." (Fisher 1992, 144) External just-in-time only functions when the customer is no longer obliged to perform receiving inspections; the supplier in this case assumes the responsibility for quality control.

– Introduction of group technology, segmentation of manufacturing, and organization along the lines of cellular manufacturing.

2. The second dimension includes social change: On the one side, concepts aimed at flexibilizing the deployment of labor so as to better utilize expensive computer-controlled machines; on the other side, teamwork, shop-floor programming, reduction of hierarchy levels, and a return of accountability to the shop level.

3. The third dimension represents – reorganization having created the conditions for their effective deployment – the introduction of technical innovations, i.e. the digitalization and electronic networking of machinery and other equipment. This includes:

– computer-aided design (CAD); this – used in design – serves to rationalize technical drawing by eliminating the need to prepare a new drawing for each workpiece; i.e. single elements are called up from a memory and displayed and manipulated on a computer screen;

– computer-aided planning (CAP), used for the direct planning of production;

– computer-aided manufacturing (CAM), a generic term for various forms of computerized manufacturing, above all computer-controlled numerical machine tools (CNC machines) and flexible manufacturing systems (FMS, i.e. the integration of a number of automatic machine tools to successively machine various stages of different workpieces);

– CAD/CAM, understood as a rule as a coupling of CAD systems with numerically controlled machine tools, the data of the workpiece designed in the CAD terminal being communicated directly to a machine tool, which then produces the workpiece required;

–   production planning and control systems (PPS), i.e. the computer-
    controlled administration of procurement and rough planning of
    the production sequence.

When firms simultaneously approach all three dimensions, this
constitutes a new best practice of industrial production that sets standards of international competitiveness. This can, of course, not mean
applying, recipe-book style, the experience of others, e.g. the Japanese;
but it does imply making use of lessons learned from other countries or
regions of the world to develop impulses for reflecting on established
procedures and ways of approaching and looking at problems. Not
being culture-specific, these organizational models can be transferred.
All the same, they are of course shaped by economic, political, and
social framework conditions as well as specific historical factors.

3.4   Building Networks

In some Western industrial countries, the relationship between the
supplier and his customer was in the past chiefly a transaction effected
via the market, an arm's-length relationship, governed by contract and
not envisaged as a long-term affiliation. A glance back nonetheless
reveals that aside from arm's-length relationships there has always
existed another type of relationship, which revealed characteristics of
a network – a long-term, trust-based relationship marked by numerous
informal contacts. This type of relationship provided opportunities to
develop inter-firm learning-by-interacting: the customer supported his
supplier in solving given problems; the supplier developed new products in close cooperation with the customer's engineers. Such close
contact encourages technological learning processes and leads to the
development of specific specialization profiles: "The fact that
Denmark is strongly specialized in dairy machines, Sweden in metal-
working and wood-cutting technology, and Norway in fishery technology cannot be explained by the general factor endowments in those
countries. Rather, we should look for the explanation in the close
interaction between producers of such machinery and a competent and
demanding domestic user sector." (Lundvall 1988, 360)

The insight that building networks of competitiveness is apt to be more beneficial than playing off suppliers against one another has gained prevalence above all in connection with the Japanese experience. As regards supply terms, the Japanese system of production differs from its Western counterparts in two respects:

- The vertical integration of the producers of end-products is much lower than that common in the West. They generally concentrate on the scale-intensive assembly of components and on final assembly. As far as possible, deliveries are made just in time, i.e. the customer is not obliged to stock them during the production process.

- The structure of the supply system in Japan is pyramid-shaped, not star-shaped; only a minority of suppliers deliver to more than one customer.

The structure of the Japanese supply system is based on the fact that the majority of major Japanese firms belong to associated corporate groups (keiretsu), which – organized for the most part around a bank and a trading company – give rise to multisector conglomerates. The formation of industrial clusters within conglomerates is facilitated by the fact that market relationships are largely replaced with in-group, usually informal, "social relationships" which make it possible to minimize transaction costs and risks. A close cooperative relationship with a major bank also diminishes their dependence on the external capital market and reduces their need to maximize short-term profits.

3.5 Company Size and Competitiveness

In the past decades, a great variety of models have shaped the discussion on management, in particular as regards the question of what type of corporate organization and size and what basic orientation are apt to offer the best promise of success. There has also been a continuing theory-level economic and industrial discussion on optimal company size, i.e. on the advantages and disadvantages of small and large firms. The discussion stimulated by the emergence of a new techno-economic paradigm which seemed to favor smaller firms.

The question of optimal company size must be left separate from any considerations of efficient plant size. The determinants of the latter are technical; the optimal plant size is seen as reached as soon as economies of scale are utilized optimally. In practice, however, suboptimal plants constitute the majority. In the USA between 3.6 % and 25.7 %, in Japan between 0.9 % and 14 % of firms in the various industries display the efficient plant size (Audretsch and Yamawaki 1991). This phenomenon can be explained by three factors: the foundation of new firms, at first small; the specialization of smaller firms in given niches; and the distinctly lower wages with which suboptimal plants compensate for their lower productivity.

The discussion on optimal company size has in recent years been marked by two experiences: on the one hand, the above-average competitiveness of Japanese corporate conglomerates; on the other hand, growing control and management problems and the exploding overhead costs with which corporations in Western ICs are struggling.

The inconsistent experiences made indicate that size in itself is often not the key category. What is more important is the manner in which a firm organizes its transactions: a major corporation that maintains primarily conflict-oriented relations with its suppliers and customers will be less competitive than a smaller company that is integrated within a properly functioning network.

Japanese conglomerates are exceptionally efficient because they constitute the basis for long-term supplier relations, because joint R&D is easier to organize, because the procurement of credit with the conglomerate's bankers is relatively simple, and because there is here a large measure of tolerance for more or less protracted initial losses. Japanese conglomerates link a dense, long-term network of relationships with a low level of organizational rigidity. This distinguishes them from conglomerates in North America and Europe in which growth of scale has been associated with a multiplication of levels of hierarchies, bureaucratization of decision-making processes, and an explosion of overhead costs.

Many of these firms today are suffering from the circumstance that they are saddled with severe weaknesses in regard to two of the four criteria specified above: due to their centralization of decision-making processes, their flexibility is as low as their responsiveness. To solve this problem, major firms in both regions are experimenting with various concepts, including

– replacement of rigid hierarchies with project organization;

– establishment of business units intended to operate as independent firms;

– stimulation of intrapreneurship, i.e. entrepreneurial behavior on the part of employees;

– restructuring of central R&D labs, which will no longer be financed as part of the overhead but will be required to canvas orders from among the business units.

These experiments are for the most part linked with efforts to slim down the firms concerned, i.e. concentration on core competence, reduction of number of employees, and cuts in vertical integration. A tendency that is taking shape here is that major firms are looking more to their own strengths, viz.

– systematic observation of worldwide market processes,

– establishment of brand names and marketing them throughout the world,

– organization of worldwide production networks (these less and less involving manufacturing plants of their own),

– organization of worldwide R&D networks, benefiting from the specific advantages of globally distributed research locations.

Similar processes are also proceeding in mid-size firms – in particular among systems suppliers – which are likewise slimming down their structures and restructuring their supply operations. Thus a structure appears to be emerging in the Western ICs which is more similar to that in Japan than it previously was: more vertically structured networks of firms, with one major firm forming the core. What will prove to be the key variable for success for failure will – as experience thus far has shown – be the extent to which major firms succeed in balancing cooperative and market relations; those which – at the intra-firm or intra-firm level – set too much store on market relations are more than likely to fail.

In contrast to the ICs, most DCs – with the exception of the Republic of Korea – are faced with the problem that their firms are hampered less by oversize and immobility than by inadequate size. It can thus make sense for major firms or groups of firms to develop (e.g. through acquisitions made in connection with the privatization of state-owned firms) during the course of the transition process. Such firms would be more in a position to organize and finance long-term export strategies; and they could also more easily present themselves to overseas firms as partners to be reckoned with (not least with an eye to technological cooperation). The danger that in this way national champions or monopolists might emerge is quite unlikely as long as markets continue to open. The greater risk is that chance conglomerates might emerge that lack a clear-cut profile – this would correspond to the failed strategy pursued by firms in the Western ICs in the 1970s. This risk can be diminished by using competition policy not to hamper the development of integrated corporations (e.g. in petrochemicals or the metal industry) but to tolerate them on the basis of a model of global competition. Apart from this, this problem is not accessible to the traditional instruments of government control and can be minimized only via new forms of control at the mesolevel.

A second possibility of coming to grips with the problem of undersized firms is to simulate the formation of clusters. Clusters of small and mid-size firms permit the development of clear-cut firm specialization profiles and the realization of economies of scale. At the same time, close cooperation between firms makes possible economies of scope. Mesoinstitutions, i.e. collective learning processes and jointly operated or utilized R&D and training facilities in the cluster context, enable even smaller firms to keep abreast of the accelerating process of technological change, without having to do without the benefits enjoyed by smaller firms as regards flexibility, responsiveness, and flat hierarchies.

4 Mesolevel Determinants – the Role of Selective Policies Toward Industry

4.1 The Significance of the Mesolevel

Within the framework of the structural adjustment of the 1980s, macroeconomic reforms and the microlevel modernization both made possible and forced by them were seen as the key to enhancing competitiveness. This view neglects the importance of expanding and building up economic regions and continuously optimizing external economies. Neoliberal theories of allocation and foreign trade point to properly functioning international technology markets and the optimal character of decentrally organized decision-making processes, rejecting active, anticipatory industrial and technology policies. However, those ICs and NICs developed most dynamically and best improved their position in the international economic hierarchy in the 1980s which succeeded in actively structuring the mesolevel.

The market alone cannot provide for an optimal structuring of locational factors. At the same time, the "development state" called for by the structuralist school has proven itself overburdened in view of the complexity of industrial production and organization when what is at issue is the development of an efficient industrial structure. Patterns of social organization of a new type and more complex patterns of public and societal governance appear to be emerging in countries which are pursuing a successful industrial location policy. The innovative interlinkage of banks, firms, and public and private intermediary institutions makes it possible to shape structures in the mesopolicy dimension with an eye to a long-term orientation. The Japanese success in particular demonstrates that creative forms of organization in this "third arena of allocation" – "between markets and hierarchies" – is a crucial factor in building national competitive advantages.

How central this neglected field of economic policy is for the development of sustained competitiveness is also revealed by the fact that a number of developing countries succeeded within the framework of structural adjustment programs in stabilizing economic framework conditions, though the expected reactivation of these economies failed to materialize (Messner 1993). The reason for this is that the industrial sites have not been developed and in some cases important locational factors were further weakened (e.g. education and R&D) in connection with the adjustment measures targeted on budget consolidation.

In the course of the past decade, the significance of the mesolevel has grown in importance as a result of radical technological-organizational change and the demise of the traditional, Fordist production paradigm. Innovation has an increasingly interactive character that rests on exchange processes organized along market-like and non-market lines. Cumulative learning effects and innovations on which systemic competitiveness is based develop via close networking on the microlevel, formal and informal cooperative relationships between firms, and sets of institutions close to the clusters in which they act. Innovation and the building of technological competence obtain under these conditions an interactive, community-related character, since, as a result of processes of learning-by-interacting and exchange processes on both a reciprocal and a market-like basis, a firm's know-how production also relies on that of its rivals, suppliers, and an innovation-friendly institutional structure. Technological competence as the foundation of the competitiveness of economies is based on difficult-to-transfer know-how pools and cumulative learning processes that emerge in the interplay among firms and institutions, giving rise to country-specific patterns, including patterns of competitive advantages.

Accordingly, the world economy now sees as competitors not decentrally operating, isolated firms but clusters or groups of firms organized in networks. The essential determinant of their development dynamics is the efficiency and flexibility of industrial sites, i.e. the existence of universities, training institutions, R&D facilities, technology information systems, private industrial organizations, and the like. Countries that, in the area of mesopolicy, see fit to do without the development of a strategic perspective as a guideline for entrepreneurial and governmental action and rely primarily on ad-hoc responses and trial-and-error processes are, in particular, underestimating

–   the importance of a timely and deliberate development of physical and – above all – immaterial infrastructure for the international competitiveness of firms,

–   the length of time required to develop human capital and technological infrastructure as central determinants of international competitiveness,

–   the negative impacts of insecurity and risk on offensive business strategies.

4.2   Innovative Forms of Efficient Public-Private Interaction

To the extent that firms manufacture more complex products, they give rise to growing demands on the local, regional, and national environment. Both the idea that government alone, as society's control center, can selectively direct technological and economic processes and the dogma which imagines that government is obliged to assume a strictly subsidiary role vis-à-vis market processes are far removed from reality. The cases of success in the world economy reveal that, between the extremes of dirigiste interventionism and a laissez-faire restricted to laying down framework conditions, there exists a broad field of action for successful policies designed to strengthen the competitiveness of industrial sites. Not unlike in industrial production, new forms of organization and governance are emerging in the sociopolitical sphere as well.

In many cases competition-relevant supply conditions emerge as a result of deregulation, privatization of state-owned enterprises, and external financial support. What is also essential is the construction of an export-oriented physical infrastructure (transportation and communication systems). But what is far more difficult is the reform and competition-oriented development of institutions in the spheres of educational, research, technology, and other industrial location policies designed to structure the mesolevel. The latter are geared to the development of an efficient institutional setting ("hardware") and rely on the interaction capacity of the public and private actors in a cluster ("software").

New forms of governance emerge: Government acts more as a coordinator, moderator, communicator between firms and their associations, science, intermediary institutions, or trade unions than in the capacity of the classical interventionist state, with the aim of promoting the dissemination of relevant information and working out joint medium- and long-term visions conceived as points of orientation for government mesopolicies and private initiatives. These new industrial location policy strategies differ fundamentally from the top-down approaches of traditional industrial policy, industrial planning, or investment guidance. The latter are today unsuitable, since in the spheres of industrial location policy and development of mesopolicies the action potentials, the know-how requisite to long-term policies and implementation capacities are distributed across a variety of governmental, private, and intermediary agencies. If, in the epoch of Fordism and highly standardized patterns of production, it was possible to successfully build vertically integrated major enterprises on the basis of centralist, government-controlled industrial planning (in the USSR, India, or even Brazil), one-dimensional, centralist patterns of regulation are doomed to failure when what is called for is the development and support of complex entrepreneurial networks and specialized institutional landscapes (Sabel 1993, Klönne et al. 1991).

"Soft governance media" (Krumbein 1991, 49) like information flows, persuasion, integration of interests, procedural definition are gaining significance as a result of these changed structural conditions. They have two functions: On the one hand, government mesopolicy is reliant on the know-how resources of and close cooperation with business, science, and other strategic actors. On the other hand, these new governance media correspond with the interactive character of innovation and the systemic character of competitiveness, since patterns of social organizations that facilitate rapid flows of information, open information channels, networked structures, and communication themselves become competitive factors.

The new forms of governance, e.g. in Japan, have gained in importance since the 1970s, when classical industrial policies (tariffs and nontariff trade barriers, export promotion via tax incentives and subsidies, R&D subsidies, formation of compulsory trusts) were prevalent (Hilpert 1993). The plans and visions presented by MITI are devised in a protracted process of communication with representatives of science and the private sector. The plans, presented at regular intervals over a period of three to four years, have no similarity whatever with directives issued by a central administration, since they are directly binding neither on businesses nor on government institutions. The visions conceived by the most important actors provide a survey of the direction of overall economic development desired and seen as right by many actors and set out consensus-based short- and medium-term goals for individual sectors which rest on a joint analysis of bottlenecks and strengths and radical changes that must be expected.

If dialogue gives rise to concrete medium-term industrial-policy visions, they are, under the conditions of rapid technological change, great instability in the capital markets, and sharp international competitive pressure, of great importance for the allocation decisions of the firms and the orientation of the governmental and public intermediary institutions at the mesolevel, despite their non-binding character. They provide guidelines for banks' decisions on lending, long-term business investment decisions, the allocation of resources in

the private sector, reorientations, and course corrections in intermediary institutions (such as training institutions and research centers).

The close interlinkage of private and public actors and the attempt to
outline future development corridors diminish insecurities, stimulate
the quest for innovations and R&D investments, and make it possible
for the firms to pursue a long-term strategy geared to growth and
winning market shares, instead of seeking primarily to maximize short-
term returns.

A further example for the growing importance of soft governance
media and the increasing relevance of functioning communications
channels between important social groups, institutions, and organizations are the "regional conferences" which have been set up in a
number of Germany's federal states, in particular in crisis regions in
which far-reaching restructuring processes are underway (e.g. North
Rhein-Westfalia; Jürgens and Krumbein 1991). Government assumes
the role of moderator, "facilitating the blending of abilities and
promoting structural networking" (Aubert 1992, 5). A good number of
the actors concerned here seek to reach agreement on future development chances of their regions, to localize bottlenecks in the modernization process, to anticipate (ecological and social) modernization
costs so as to be able to reduce them, thus creating orientations for
political and entrepreneurial decision-making. In the regions, complex
networks emerge, integrating business organizations, trade unions,
industrial associations, local administrations, technology institutes, and
universities. These interpose themselves between state and market,
elaborate visions – or, expressed more pragmatically: scenarios – for
regional development, pave the way for strategic decisions of far-
reaching scope, and break the ground for non-statist political governance of economic restructuring programs and an active and anticipatory shaping of structures.

These new network-like industrial- and technology-policy approaches
thus differ clearly on the one hand from hierarchic, one-sidedly statist
governance concepts (industrial planning) and on the other hand from
purely free-market solutions. The development of new patterns of

social organization and "autonomy-compatible techniques of intervention and regulation" (Scharpf 1992) at the mesolevel facilitate the
governance and shaping of market processes and reduce the weaknesses of pure market mechanism and statist planning. These mechanisms make it possible to relieve government's burden by shifting
decision-making processes into intermediary arenas, ensure a higher
degree of information availability, heighten the legitimacy of government decisions, and optimize the utilization of social creativity by
mobilizing the problem-solving capacities of strategically important
actors. They do, however, presuppose on the part of social actors a
capacity to compromise, to perform and learn, and to accept transformation. The conditions for an efficient mesopolicy are difficult in
many countries as a result of social polarizations and a lack of experience in communication and interaction between private and public
actors or corporative structures with a rentist orientation.

4.3   The Importance of Industrial Clusters and Networks
at the Regional and National Level

Aside from general innovation-friendly framework conditions, what is
required to develop dynamic competitive advantages are specific,
selective mesopolicies. Selectivity at the mesolevel, instead of the
widespread "pork-barrel" approach to promotion, aims at "strengthening the strong" with an eye to building, as rapidly as possible, dynamic industrial centers and efficient industrial sites that communicate
their effects to less developed areas.

Selectivity aims at three levels:

—   concentration of mesopolicies on industrial clusters with development potential;

—   at the cluster level, development of a powerful cluster environment, i.e. cluster-related innovation-friendly framework conditions, instruments to support best performers (picking the winners), so as to enable them to connect up with the international
best practice, and the building of structures aimed at smoothing

the path of firms with development potential toward the level held
by the group of best performers;

- strengthening of developing regions in which dynamic groups of
  firms or clusters are emerging.

Policies aimed at shaping the mesolevel have a national and a
regional/local dimension. At the national level, mesopolicies are
geared to developing physical infrastructures tailored to the clusters
(transportation: ports, rail and road networks; telecommunications;
supply and disposal systems: energy, water/waste water, refuse) and
immaterial infrastructures (building of educational systems, etc.). What
is furthermore important are selective and active foreign trade policies
(including strategies for tapping new markets) and an active body in
charge of representing interests at the international level (e.g. against
IC protectionism). Apart from this selective improvement of the
national mesolevel, cluster-specific policies at the regional and local
level are also of significance.

The latter are essential in view of the fact that the process of clustering
is most dynamic in regionally limited areas. Proximity of the actors
involved in clusters is an essential productive force, while the 1970s
and 1980s discussions on the "new international division of labor"
(Fröbel, Heinrichs and Kreye 1977) were dominated by the idea that
industrial siting (and thus proximity) would lose significance as an
important competitive factor due to investment decisions of multi-
national corporations oriented in terms of wage cost advantages
(worldwide sourcing). The shift of the production paradigm from
standardized to flexible mass production and the interactive character
of innovation have heightened the importance of industrial location as
a factor influencing the competitiveness of firms.

In the process of trade liberalization, dynamic export firms (often in
proximity to resources) emerge in some regions. Local and regional
governments have a great role to play in systematically improving the
business environment in export regions. In areas such as university
education and the founding of new or reorientation of existing

faculties, industrial infrastructure, local and regional research and training institutions, and information channels, local and regional "governments" gain in significance vis-à-vis central government. It is here that decisions touching directly upon industrial location are made and structural policies implemented.

In regions displaying dynamic development, the efficiency of firms is enhanced by economies of agglomeration. Agglomeration advantages materialize to the extent that firms that produce at a properly developed site, with a good manpower potential, efficient suppliers, and a good supply of information – i.e. firms in a position to turn external economies to account – have lower production costs than the same firms outside such industrial sites.

In other words, the necessity of decentralizing political decision-making and a redefinition of the competences of national and regional and local policy instances derives from the growing significance of spatiostructural factors for the competitiveness of firms. Traditional industrial policies, formulated far from industrial sites in the planning ministries of capitals, are obsolete. Extension of the competence and financial latitudes of regional and local administration has a crucial role to play within the framework of government reform. The goal is to build institutional structures that make it possible to shape the structures in the local and regional industrial sites (structuring from below). Regional structuring is geared to strengthening the inter-firm linkages between firms, shaping the inter-firm space, promoting close linkages between industry and services, and building interactional relationships between the regional and the national levels (Porter 1990).

Decentralization must not be misunderstood as a schematic shift of responsibility to lower decision-making levels or as a decoupling process between regions and state (Kochen and Deutsch 1980). Just as in modern corporations the greater autonomy of profit centers implies not abolishing top corporate management but expanding control capacities and changing tasks for central management (network organizers and development of strategic visions for the firm as a whole instead of central control over all corporate sectors), in the public sector, too, effective decentralization depends on complementary changes at the central level (Scharpf 1992). Central government remains important as the agency responsible for ensuring an integration of dynamic agglomerative interlinkages to form a national development strategy, initiating productive feedback loops between local and regional sites, accelerating the progress of building a national infrastructure, and implementing an active external trade policy (structuring from above).

A structuring of the mesolevel geared to a close interlinkage between firms and surrounding institutions is the permanent task facing the public and private sectors. It is a protracted process that places great demands on government's control and steering capacity at the national, regional, and local level in close connection with other strategic actors. Even though many developing countries have training, technology, financial, and marketing institutions, these institutions have often failed to contribute to enhancing the competitiveness of firms. The interaction and communication links between firms and the institutions surrounding them are often so weak that no efficient and innovative structures emerge. Many countries will be concerned with transforming existing institutions in such a way as to enable these institutions to provide any services at all to industry and society. What is important is that mesopolicy be understood as a cross-sectional task of public and private actors, aimed at continuity in improving locational conditions. The crucial factor is to link individual measures in such a way as to shape interlinkage-oriented mesopolicies. A properly structured mesolevel is important not only to enhancing and safeguarding international competitiveness, it is at the same time the basis of any effective implementation of flanking social and environmental policies.

4.4   Training and Advanced Training

Economic structuring cannot succeed without the formation of coherent social structures. During the phase of inward orientation, the development of industrial and educational systems was characterized by quantitative expansion. When market forces are strengthened without at the same time strengthening social structures, competitive orientation cannot not proceed in the direction of success. Reform and development of educational systems must be geared to achieving three goals: orientation toward social values, intensification of broad social effects, and preparation for new levels of qualification.

1. Orientation of education in terms of social values: For social and economic reasons, a value orientation is crucial that aims at consensus-based cooperation, joint responsibility and readiness to deal with conflicts, communicative cooperation and teamwork, and an active and autonomous process of lifelong learning. These primary educational goals encourage social integration and meet the requirements of industry. The new production paradigm calls for a type of employee who is flexible, prepared to cooperate, quality-conscious, and accustomed to learning, and who is in possession of practical voca-tional competence and marked communicative skills and able to think in broader contexts. The primary educational goals are most difficult to achieve in fragmented societies, although they constitute a condition for social consensus and any concerted social action.

2. Intensification of broad social effects: Any achievement of broad social effects is improved by forming focal points in the fields of primary education and industrial vocational training. Vocational qualification can, according to needs, be tailored to the specific demands of the informal sector, technical-manual training, or the training of skilled workers in the competition-oriented industrial segments.

Other factors also contribute to achieving broad social effects:

- literacy programs that at the same time encourage technical understanding,

- media with preparatory educational or vocational-training programs, or

– university scholarships in fields relevant to the international competitiveness of the economy.

3. Preparation for new qualification profiles: This will for the most part first emphasize intensification of intra-firm training and advanced training. Enterprises that make use of the new concepts of industrial organization intensify training. Due to low wage costs, even protracted courses can be financed with an eye to familiarizing workforces with the latest quality and lean-manufacturing systems. In view of already-high – and increasing – qualification requirements, a rapid transition to the training of apprentices is important in competition-oriented economic segments. Moreover, specialization will proceed, far more than during the phase of Taylorist mass production, via advanced vocational training ("learning by doing" plus short intra-firm or external training courses).

At the same time, however, the transition to flexible mass production requires a parallel reform of general education and vocational training:

– on the one hand, a high level of average general education, e.g. at the expense of public support for university education, as the basis of higher vocational qualification;

– on the other hand, overcoming the traditional opposition between theory and practice in inter-firm vocational training geared to specific needs (Anglo-Saxon discussion: integration of education and training; German discussion: encouragement of a dual system in which practical training is conducted intra-firm).

What is important in vocational schools is not only to increase specific performance but also to take into consideration requirements going above and beyond individual subjects. It is therefore recommendable to link the basic qualification provided by one vocational field (e.g. metal-working) with overlapping forms of learning and acquiring and processing information, working with computers and practicing team-work techniques (specialized and despecialized vocational training).

The protracted transition from mass production organized along hierarchic Taylorist lines to flexible mass production on the model of lean production places great demands on education and educational research. This is true in view of the task of testing various concepts of business organization (via combinational patterns of hierarchic organization of work processes and horizontal control on the operational level with autonomous units and teamwork), and because such concepts are gaining prevalence not only in industrial firms, but will also, in tendency, change the organization of work in the services sectors, including the public sector.

4. Regulation toward the end of system integration: Educational reforms will be geared to international standards and the requirements placed by new concepts of organization and production, though they will at the same time take account of country-specific structures and needs. A gradual modus operandi and point-by-point approaches ought form the very outset to be tied into a system perspective, e.g. in terms of a system of vocational training. Core elements of the reform and development of education are:

– government regulation which increases the importance of education and research with an eye to economic and social concerns,

– concentration on strengthening managerial capacities in educational institutions so as to provide for responsible institutional management,

– sustaining the approach via educational research institutions and proposals advanced by intermediary organizations, above all of industry,

– fine-tuning among central and decentral educational institutions and ensuring competition between public- and private-sector institutions at higher levels of qualification, and

– linking quantitative expansion and improvement of quality with a more pronounced practical orientation.

5. Step-by-step expansion of focus: Educational systems are expanded gradually and in close coordination with the needs of the economy. Urgent requirements include:

– rehabilitation of existing educational institutions,

– provision of meals in the educational institutions and solution of transportation problems,

– development of focal points in industrial vocational training in segments with a larger demand for skilled labor and participatory interest and willingness to provide funding on the part of industrial associations,

– expansion of technical colleges that train medium-level technical staff and management,

– concentration in universities on economics, natural sciences and engineering, and computer sciences, and

– priority expansion of technical universities and their postgraduate training in areas of qualification serving to improve technological competence and international competitiveness.

6. Partnership between government and industry: The new demands placed on industry can be met only if there is close cooperation between government, educational institutions, research, and industry. This is all the more so as they can be met only in the course of a protracted transitional process that will involve a great measure of sectoral and regional differentiation and will on the whole change the ways in which people live and work. A cooperatively structured educational system is of great significance for these reasons.

In view of its regulatory competence, government is responsible for the direction that education on the whole will take as well as for a high level of average general education. For instance, government is responsible for preventing or counteracting such undesirable developments as the emergence of a great number of small private universities of low quality. In the field of advanced vocational qualification, government should involve all aspects of the economy (self-administered organizations like chambers of industry and commerce and trade guilds), including, if possible the trade unions, in developing and implementing a concept. Joint responsibility implies industry's taking a share in vocational training and bearing a share of the financial burden. As a rule, industry's share in vocational training is inadequate. In higher education there is competition. Studying implies paying tuition. Cooperation between government and the economy can provide some of the required funding.

7. Concrete cooperation among education, research, and industry: Establishing linkages between the various subsystems involves:

- courses of practical training,

- practical relevance of college theses, in particular doctoral dissertations, to best practice issues facing industry (for which, in turn, industry can offer scholarships),

- mobility of experts between educational and research institutions and industry,

- research and consultation projects that contribute toward supplying laboratories and workshops with working assets,

- advanced training of scientists, in particular of engineers, abroad, and

- repatriation programs and invitations addressed to experts working abroad, in collaboration between universities and industry.

Concrete cooperation contributes to a needs-oriented vocational training, a rapid placement of university graduates in the economy, a joint testing of dialogue techniques and network-building, and improvement of the world-market competence of the economy. The potential of institutions of higher learning to support the development of technological competence and improvement of the economy's international competitiveness via research, consultancy, and other circumstances is significant, although it has until now for the most part been underutilized. This potential grows when efforts are roughly coordinated with non-academic research institutions and industry, which can also avoid any reduplication of the efforts undertaken. If the intention is to focus on knowledge-intensive technologies in the universities so as to further the advance of science in technology-intensive industries, a clear-cut rise in public spending for education and research will prove unavoidable.

8. Regional cooperation in education and research: Regional coordination of vocational training and academic education and R&D cooperation can be deepened via cooperation between smaller neighboring states (e.g. Central America), and intensified via an orientation in terms of industry-relevant focal points (e.g. advanced technical and commercial training, post-graduate scholarships in natural sciences and engineering). Regional know-how in the field of new technologies (computer sciences, biotechnology) can be clustered to form regional centers of excellence. Regional educational and research networks contribute toward concentrating forces in priority industry-relevant fields. Obstructions to interaction among universities, R&D institutions, and firms from different countries should be dismantled.

4.5   Research and Technology

In most DCs technology policy has in the past contributed little to diminishing the technological gap and, in particular, to upgrading industry in technological terms. Although technology institutes and universities have been developed in many DCs, they have lacked relevance to the problems facing the economy, and their links to the productive sector have been weak. Unlike the case in the ICs and a few advanced DCs, no national system of innovation has emerged.

Technological networks of firms, universities, and research institutions have emerged where firms are engaged in sharp competition in innovation, quality, and meeting deadlines. This was, however, hardly the case in most DCs in the past; technology policy often proceeded on false premises.

This is not to say that in those countries that pursued an inward-looking strategy there was no such thing as technological learning processes. But the problem was that the learning processes were distorted. They aimed less at improving economic efficiency than at adjusting to conditions presented by narrow domestic markets. "Typical R&D efforts would be determined by the need to use different raw materials, scale down (to smaller) plant size, diversify the product mix, change the product design, use simpler, more universal, less automated and lower capacity machinery, stretch out the capacity of existing equipment, etc." (Teitel 1987, 109)

It was thus an idiosyncratic process of improvement and adjustment to a distorted environment. There is little to indicate that optimization as a means of adjustment to distorted conditions is an intermediate stage on the road to international efficiency. On the contrary: it was a process of optimization that led in a different direction and often increased the disparity of firms vis-à-vis the international level of efficiency. Technology institutions and universities – for the most part geared to models imported from ICs – had little more than a minor role to play in this process.

A further fallacy also played a role in the past: the establishment of technology institutions was based on the technology-push model, according to which breakthroughs in basic research provide impulses to applied research, which these in turn pass on to product development. In fact, however, research and development is for the most part an interactive process; and it is frequently not scientific breakthroughs that impel technological progress, but, on the contrary, technological breakthroughs that induce scientific research, which then seeks to interpret the essence and foundations of a technology already in use.

In contrast to this, a national system of innovation emerged in connection with the industrialization process in most ICs and in successful DCs. An efficient system of innovation is characterized by the fact that, above and beyond the level of individual, locally limited clusters, technological networks emerge between industrial and services firms, R&D and training institutions, and public-sector agencies. It is less the size than the density of networked relationships that decides on the success of a system of innovation. A well-organized system of innovation "may enable a country with rather limited resources nevertheless to make very rapid progress through appropriate combinations of imported technology and local adaptation and development. On the other hand, weaknesses in the national system of innovation may lead to more abundant resources being squandered in the pursuit of inappropriate objectives or use of ineffective methods." (Freeman 1987, 3)

Networks give rise to technological externalities – either intentionally (e.g. on the basis of contractual relationships between supplier and customer or firm and research institute) or unintentionally (via manpower fluctuation, informal exchange of information, and the like). They are the prime example for positive external effects through which industry on the whole stands to gain more than individual firms lose; in most cases the benefit the individual firm derives from information stemming from other sources is even greater than the damage due to information "leaks". The disadvantage implied by the circumstance that an individual firm is no longer able to enjoy the exclusive yield of its innovations is more than compensated for by the heightened competitiveness of the network; a network permits "a collective rather than an individual form of rent appropriation and requires social and cultural preconditions which some nations possess more widely than others." (OECD 1992, 84)

The existence of pronounced technological externalities makes possible rapid interactive, cumulative learning processes (Rosenberg 1982, 120 ff) in the course of which a network of firms and institutions comes to master, and translate into market success, technological process and product innovations far faster than can isolated firms sited differently. The existence of continuous cumulative learning processes can lead to situations in which a country (more exactly: given industries in a country) can build up absolute competitive advantages (Dosi, Pavitt and Soete 1990, 148 ff). This type of absolute advantage rests not on static comparative advantages; rather, it is based on the capacity of a network of firms to hold, or even to build up, a lead it has once achieved. Empirical research has shown that technological leads can be sustained over a longer period of time. This explanatory model illustrates "why, since the late 1970s, some OECD countries have run long-term, almost permanent trade surpluses and other almost equally permanent deficits." (OECD 1992, 251)

Successful national systems of innovation that may even build up absolute competitive advantages are characterized in particular by a type of government which (at the level of central, provincial, and local government) stimulates and fosters the building of systemic competitiveness. In doing so, it avails itself of the following instruments:

–   encouragement of basic and applied research in universities as well as in major public- and private-sector research institutions;

–   stimulation of technology diffusion (information and advisory institutions, industry-specific demonstration centers, technology promotion centers);

–   encouragement of industry R&D (indirect and specific promotion, R&D interlinkages, venture capital);

–   public procurement policy;

–   targeting, long-term visions, technology assessment, and regional technology dialogues, government playing more the role of initiator and moderator than pioneer.

4.6   Policies and Institutions in Trade

In DCs, trade policy is faced with two challenges: the implementation of an intelligent import policy and an effective policy of export promotion.

Many DCs have radically opened up to the world market in connection with structural adjustment programs, which has led in the manufacturing industries to a process of exaggerated adjustment. More promising is a gradual strategy of opening in which external protection is gradually reduced to the internationally accepted level of 10-15 % within a period of three to four years.

Successful countries are characterized by a selective import policy. They not only stimulate exports by removing tariffs and levies on imported pre-products and, in some cases, investment goods (drawback). They also pursue a consistent policy of infant industry protection oriented in terms of clear-cut performance criteria and limited in time.

1. **Encouragement of exports** is promoted in many DCs by a variety of different export-related institutions: trading firms/TCs, trade promotion agencies, information services. These are supplemented by certain infrastructural preconditions and conditions and institutions in the broader sense of the term, e.g. export-related import regulation. Successful countries differ from less successful ones in terms of the effective organization of these institutions, but above all in terms of the articulation and creation of cumulative effects among institutions. Enterprises are able to asserts themselves in the world market in particular when they are accorded concerted support by the institutions named.

2. **Trading firms**: TCs in the ICs (sogo shoshas, and other, similar foreign-trade and marketing establishments) make up for up to 20 % of the industrial goods exported by developing countries. In some Latin American countries, they also pool the agricultural produce of SMEs for export; the best known example is the *fruticultura de exportación* in Chile. They arrange for sea freight and use their international connections to diversify export markets. They frequently have close relations to financial institutions; in some cases they even provide credit of their own. The activities of the TCs also have other important secondary effects:

–   They provide local producers with soft technologies (design, adaptation to different taste preferences, quality control).

–   They give rise to rapid modernization of suppliers as well, e.g. in the field of packaging materials.

– They commission scientific studies at local universities.

– They send groups of local experts abroad for advanced training, e.g. from Chile to California.

– They finance consulting services on economic, organizational, and technical problems.

– They push through rapid modernization of the local transportation sector and port facilities.

Beside the foreign marketing organizations, existing or new local *empresas exportadoras* are growing in significance in Latin America, some of which have already grown to a considerable size. As a result of producer firms' disadvantages in scale and know-how, and because the countries of the region can now be integrated in the global telecommunications systems of the TCs, "indirect export" of this type, with its "system integration" via a foreign trading company, will continue to grow in importance. One other reason why this is the case is that the organizational and management services provided by the trading firms, in particular trade management, are being complemented by more and more service functions (supply of spare parts, warranty services, customer service) as well as the handling of contra trans-actions. One visible disadvantage is that export trading firms can permanently restrict the initiative and the learning processes of the firms participating in them.

3. **Export consortia**: "Direct export" by SMEs can be transacted via consortia. These are an independent form of export cooperation, often limited in time. Such consortia serve to transact jointly production tasks involving major lot sizes, e.g. department store chains, mail order establishments, or the like, in ICs. These consortia, e.g. in the shoe or garment industries, do not as a rule exist on a permanent basis. In many countries it appears that they are being replaced by TCs, which are much more in a position to contribute to increasing the efficiency of local producers and provide for more continuity through follow-up orders. In Columbia, the formation of company groups below the merger level ("grupos solidarios"), aimed at improving the cost

structure of production, is encouraged by government, although this practice has yet to achieve any particular significance.

4. **Trade promotion agencies**: Successful trade promotion agencies meet four criteria: They are taken seriously and supported by firms; they are adequately funded; they employ qualified staff, who receive salaries usual in the market; they have a certain measure of autonomy.

Very few trade promotion agencies in DCs meet these criteria, which is why most of them are relatively unsuccessful; this is one further example for the failure of government institutions in inward-looking societies. In particular, there are six factors that guarantee failure:

– "the unsuitability of government employees to the task,

– the inflexibility of government procedures on expenditures and staffing,

– the confusion of purpose resulting from the assumption of regulatory and administrative roles,

– the perpetuation of wrong attitudes and strategies,

– misguided evenhandedness among potential export firms and producers that prevents a focused approach and limits the information given to potential importers, and

– the neglect of the development of commercial services." (Keesing and Singer 1992, 53)

An additional factor is that existing government agencies have a legal monopoly and therefore do not only not function properly, but furthermore obstruct the emergence of efficient private agencies.

5. **Information services**: One effect of the diffusion of new, computer-based technology is that many of the classical print media are becoming obsolete. This is especially true for market information. Technological change is attended by structural change: private firms have increasingly come to see a lucrative market in the transmission of information. The consequence is that, as more timely and systematic

information becomes available, access prices rise. This has two implications for DCs. On the one hand, they need a low-cost access to the international telecommunications system, for only in this way can they avail themselves of information sources in other counties. On the other hand, it has a dysfunctional impact when legal barriers bar domestic or foreign firms from this field.

6. **Infrastructure**: High domestic transportation costs (frequently a result of inefficient road-bound transportation systems), unreliable transportation systems and inadequate port capacities, and ineffective and inefficient ports are in many DCs a severe export obstacle.[4] By way of contrast, successful DCs are characterized by especially efficient ports. Thus, for instance, Singapore has the largest handling capacity of all ports of the world. This position is due not only to its geographical situation but also to its exceptional efficiency: large container ships can be handled (unloaded, loaded, refueled, etc.) within a period of only nine hours. The ports of Hong Kong and Kaohsiung (Taiwan) are not far behind.

4.7   Industrial Financing and Financial Export Incentives

In financing their activities, the majority of industrial firms in most DCs have in the past been confronted with five problems:

-   a selective lending policy of private and public commercial banks, but also of development banks, which have preferred major private and public firms, so that no long-term financing has been available to other firms;

-   exaggerated demands for collateral;

-   an underdeveloped stock exchange, which has prevented most firms from issuing stock;

-   high interest rates for working capital on the part of banks or for borrowing in the informal sector;

-   a lack of export-finance institutions.

SMEs have thus in the past had to rely on self-financing; this on the one hand implied recourse to owner savings or mobilization of capital among family members; on the other hand, it necessarily gave rise to mark-up pricing to make it possible to finance investments from cash-flow.

A fundamental change of the financial sector accompanies the opening of economies. The banking system – sometimes constrained by the entry to the market of foreign institutions – is modernized, thus improving and diversifying the opportunities of financing open to firms. Competition between banks stimulates efforts to increase efficiency, thus leading to lower costs in the financial sector and the emergence of additional financing opportunities; transaction margins decrease, administrative costs for small portfolios fall, short-term mentalities and risk aversion give way to an interest in cooperation, including with SMEs.

By consistently utilizing the opportunities afforded them by electronic banking, major firms can diversify their sources of financing, combine different financing instruments, and pursue a professional strategy of liquidity and foreign-exchange management. This, however, diminishes the banks' yields from the zero-interest transfers and cash stocks floating in the banking system and increases their incentive to diversify their customer base – not least in the direction of SMEs. It can be observed in several Latin American countries that banks are discovering SMEs as new clients, especially as they can in this way diversify their risks; electronic banking moreover makes it possible for them to lower their costs for transactions with small clients.

Aside from traditional credit, banks and specialized institutions increasingly support firms in utilizing other forms of financing (Buitelaar, Mertens and Schulz 1992, 57 ff).

1. **Leasing**: Here, by paying a leasing fee, a firm acquires the right to use a given equipment for a given period of time. One advantage of this over financing investments via credit is that the firms concerned needs not provide collateral. In Latin America, for instance, this

instrument has been in common use since the end of the 1960s; but leasing firms have tended to focus their leasing business on large firms. An extension of this business to include SMEs would imply considerable expansion potential.

2. **Bonds**: Mid-size and larger firms in particular are in a position to finance their business via bonds. In Latin America, for instance, working capital is increasingly financed via bonds with a maximum maturity period of three months; these bonds are issued via securities markets or sold directly to institutional investors. They offer sizable interest-rate advantages as compared with bank loans.

3. **Collateral funds and partnership structures**: For SMEs, it is often particularly difficult to provide collateral when borrowing. This problem is today solved in a number of DCs in two different ways. Collateral funds serve as security for SMEs to borrow working capital; the multiplication factor usually starts at 10 and increases to 25 over the course of several years. The funds cover up to 80 % of a credit. The greater part of the funding in most cases stems from government SME promotion programs, although these funds for the most part operate independently – not least because they function well only when they are able to build up a good measure of credibility and professional standing and establish clear-cut rules. Current financing is conducted via a provision fee paid by businesses making use of the funds. Partnership structures, on the other hand, are characterized by the fact that in this case it is the firms themselves that raise and administer the money for the guarantee fund.

4. **Factoring**: The sale of claims to specialized factoring firms is a form of financing which is customary in ICs but has as yet not become widespread in DCs. It would therefore be useful and appropriate to found factoring firms or encourage international factoring firms to set up branch organizations.

5. **Export financing**: Two instruments used to facilitate exports have been gaining prevalence; many DCs, however, have as yet made too little use of them. One instrument is the provision, at the national level,

of letters of credit (domestic letters of credit in Republic of Korea, for example), an instrument that has thus far found too little use; e.g. in Latin America only 25 % of exports are transacted via L/Cs. What is at stake here in particular is to ease for "indirect importers", i.e. the suppliers of export firms (which often have difficulty in providing security) access to working capital. The second instrument is establishment of export credit insurance organizations with which exporters can insure their transactions against payment losses. Founding a specialized export finance bank is an daunting firm; but all successful exporting nations have undertaken this effort, because the benefits involved far outweigh the costs.

6. **Stock exchanges**: In many DCs, particularly in East Asia and Latin America, the business transacted at stock exchanges has developed dynamically in recent years. But this should not obscure the fact that it is for the most part the stock of a small group of major firms that is traded here. It would thus in future be possible for mid-size firms to broaden their capital base by entering the stock exchange.

7. **Financing via venture capital**: in several ICs and a lesser number of advanced DCs, venture-capital financing has proven to be an interesting instrument for founding technology-oriented firms. The lenders here bet that the profits from a successful new firm will compensate for the losses incurred from a number of flops. Venture-capital funds are, however, successful only when they are competently managed, i.e. in a position to distinguish between more and less promising business concepts. For new technology-oriented firms, venture-capital financing is often the only possibility to obtain external funding, since they are unable to provide adequate collateral.

8. **Pension funds and insurance firms**: Pension funds and insurance firms in DCs chiefly invest their capital in government bonds; a small share of it is, however, occasionally invested in housing construction. For industrial firms, they are a source of capital that has thus far remained largely untapped.

9. **International financing:** Once the economic performance of the highly indebted countries had improved, a number of major firms from these countries again succeeded in gaining access to the international capital markets. They have often been able to procure capital at interest rates much lower the domestic rates by issuing bonds on the international capital market.

SMEs often view business forms such as leasing with skepticism, failing to comprehend the benefits involved or regarding the possession of capital goods as a value per se. For SMEs, it is therefore essential to disseminate information about new financing instruments, to practice using new financing techniques, and to improve their financial management. Here, specialized institutions can be of use which actively market these instruments among SMEs while being subject to clear-cut performance indicators.

Financial-sector reforms are concerned with creating the conditions that permit firms – and in particular SMEs – to gain access to diversified forms of investment financing. One important aspect of this is that domestic markets be opened to foreigners. Just as in the case of import policy, any too rapid, radical opening in financial-sector policy can be dysfunctional. Any opening to foreign banks looking for long-term investment opportunities should be welcome, especially since they step up the performance pressure on national banking systems. On the other hand, caution should be exercised in opening stock exchanges to foreign investors. As long as a stock exchange remains under-developed, i.e. relatively few securities are traded there, an inflow of foreign capital will lead to rapid price advances. But, as the experience of recent years has shown, the lion's share of this is speculative capital. If is withdrawn abruptly, the result can be a crash, an event that is detrimental to the institution's reputation as well as the to willingness of as yet unlisted firms to issue stock. What is therefore preferable are special investment opportunities for foreign investors, e.g. capital funds, administered by foreign branches of national banks.

4.8   Environmental Policy

The resource- and energy-intensive industrialization hitherto pursued
has exacerbated the problem that the practice of resource utilization,
i.e. attitudes toward nature, set going with an eye to augmenting
material welfare now threatens to destroy the foundations of life. The
problem in DCs is even more intractable in that the process of opening
and the constraint on many developing countries to earn foreign
exchange in order to repay their foreign debt can lead to overutilization
of resources and externalization of ecological costs (e.g. uncontrolled
emissions). This objective pressure must be relieved via external
measures (debt relief, reduction of protectionism, ecologically oriented
shaping of WTO) and internal environmental policies. What is called
for is a prevention-oriented environmental policy geared to combating
and avoiding ecological damage and providing incentives for national
innovativeness aimed at the development of ecologically compatible
forms of production. Any future-oriented environmental strategy rests
on visions, institutions, and instruments geared to altering existing
practices vis-à-vis nature. It must be an integral component of
industrialization strategies.

Building a national setting adequate to shaping the environmental
dimension of industrial competitiveness aims at:

1. **Reduction of unregulated ecological burdens**: internationally
available environmentally sound technologies have scarcely been used
within the framework of inward-looking resource- and energy-
intensive industrialization, e.g. in Latin America, or in the former
socialist countries. In addition, approaches to industrialization have
often stalled in resource- and energy-intensive heavy industries. This
has, accordingly, given rise to unregulated ecological burdens (air
pollution and soil contamination, inefficient energy systems) which
must be reduced.

2. **Support for systemic reorganization efforts at the firm level** that
take ecological considerations into account: the process of restructuring industry toward the world market makes it possible to gear

operations to internationally accepted best practices in environmental technologies and appropriate patterns of organization oriented toward decoupling production and the consumption of environmentally valuable resources. It would, for instance, be possible to install in industrial plants integrated power-heat equipment that could reduce industrial energy consumption by up to 90 %. In many ICs (e.g. in Germany), the introduction of these technologies is progressing slowly, since oligopolistic supply structures in the energy sector are obstructing the process of change. DCs could make more rapid progress here.

3. **Increase of energy efficiency**: the World Watch Institute has pointed out that it would be possible for ICs to triple their energy efficiency on the basis of existing best-practice technologies.

> "Developing countries can improve their energy efficiency by an even greater amount, since design changes from the start allow processes of leapfrogging, while strengthening their economies. One example: Third World power plants consume as much as 44 percent more fuel per kilowatt-hour than those in ICs, while transmission and distribution losses are three to four times higher. A recent study suggests that comprehensive efforts to improve energy efficiency could save the DCs $ 30 billion annually and eliminate the projected need for 500 000 megawatts of power by 2025." (Brocon et al. 1991, 37)

Future-oriented environmental policy is shaped by government environmental authorities and relies on effective social actors:

–   Industrial associations could provide (e.g. via information in the field of intra-firm environmental protection) the means of focusing entrepreneurial expertise and creativity on solving the environmental problems caused by industry. The trade unions, too, could contribute to improving environmental conditions by integrating environmental issues in their action plans (e.g. approaches to factors in firms which are detrimental to health and the environment).

–   Application-oriented science (universities, private research institutions, technology institutions) can develop environmental-policy programs and conceptions and provide support in formulating targets and standards of environmental policy and selecting and applying such instruments and measures. What is important for DCs is to have information on the know-how available in ICs and be able to apply it to their own conditions.

–   Consumer organizations can, through their information and consulting work, influence the environment-related awareness and behavior of the population and generate pressure on firms to make allowance for environmental criteria as quality features of their products.

–   Private environmental associations can promote ecological awareness and influence environmental policy, e.g. by issuing position papers and holding hearings on important ecologically relevant projects and legislation.

The set of instruments available to environmental policy includes regulations and prohibitions, structural-policy measures and a variety of information and advisory services:

–   The environmental liability anchored in law can call to account those responsible for causing ecological damage.

–   Environmental compatibility tests can be used to determine and assess, comprehensively and at an early date, whether proposed projects, public or private, can be approved as ecologically sound.

–   Product standards set by panels recruited from industry and environmental authorities can define the ecological demand placed on products. Environmental symbols and quality ratings have proven to be an interesting incentive for firms.

–   Spatial planning (spatial structuring, transportation planning, establishment of industrial zones, landscape planning) can contribute to avoiding and reducing material environmental burdens and using land economically and sparingly.

–   Important economic incentives aimed at reducing ecological burdens can be provided by control levies exacted on emissions (e.g. waste water levy, CO_2 levy) and by increasingly focusing on ecological aspects in shaping taxation policies. What might furthermore be of importance is depreciation regulations or low-interest credit programs for the environmental modernization of firms.

–   For the purpose of setting environmental goals and priorities and checking on the success of environmental measures, what is needed is information on the level and development of the state of the environment and the economic costs caused by ecological damage. Environmental reporting is an important means to this end.

Most DCs (and many ICs) lack these institutional structures for developing a modern environmental policy. The set of policies outlined and an ecologically shaped mesolevel would contribute to overcoming the merely flanking character of the environmental policy of the past and change the environmental dimension, in the sense of the "revolution in ecological efficiency" called for by the World Watch Institute, into an integral component of systemic competitiveness.

Part III How to Make Industry Competitive: Guidelines for Key Decision-Makers

1   Development of Competitive Strength as a Step-by-Step Process

Part II discussed the individual determinants of systemic competitiveness at the three system levels. Part III will explore the scopes of action open to developing countries to meet the demands posed by systemic competitiveness.

1.1   Transition from an Inward-Looking to a World-Market-Oriented Strategy

One important consideration in the transitional phase leading from an inward-looking strategy to one keyed to the world market is not to lose sight of the interdependence of the individual reform steps initiated, in this way implementing, as rapidly as possible, a critical mass of the most urgent reforms:

1. One crucial initial step is to stabilize and to learn to work with the new market- and world-market-oriented macropolicy. This is essential to safeguard stable macroeconomic framework conditions so as to set in motion a process entailing the development of systemic competitiveness. The first attempt will not necessarily prove successful in every country.

2. Macropolicy alone is not adequate to develop market- and world-market-oriented framework conditions. Instead, the transitional phase

should be used to alter the overall framework; the following elements are significant here:

- to develop the functional conditions of a market economy (private ownership, freedom of contract, freedom of competition, free price formation, the rule of law);

- to reform the state sector: central government, regions, and communities have to work to develop a new mutual relationship, build up professional bureaucracies, and, by defining a strict and clear-cut division of functions, set the stage for interlinkage between the most important groups of relevant actors.

- to initiate the privatization of state-owned firms, industrial rehabilitation programs, and the conversion of arms industries, trying to use this to strengthen national private firms and attract foreign direct investment. What is aimed for is a level of regulation conducive to competition and a level of external protection that provides incentives for adjustment, but without losing sight of the economy's response potential.

- to reduce transportation, energy, and communications costs; to establish a flexible labor market; to reform the sectors of education/training, technology, and finance; to improve export-oriented organization. Factors contributing to strengthening competitiveness also include debt reprogramming, new inflows of capital (not least the repatriation of flight capital), retrenchment of high-interest policies and exaggerated exchange rates (in connection with a successful anti-inflation program), and an adjustment of the financial sector to the needs of the productive sector.

- The state must make efforts to bring runaway slow variables under control (population growth, internal migration, crime, the drugs trade, and environmental degradation stemming from wasteful exploitation of natural resources). It must also implement policies aimed at alleviating absolute poverty and ensuring the precedence of "increased productivity before wage hikes".

- By promoting (sub)regional integration the state can open up the way to an exploitation of greater market dimensions, thus fostering growing returns to scale and the formation of regional spatial-economic structures.

3. The first phase of export orientation is dominated by efforts to increase the efficiency of existing firms capable of modernization. There exist as a rule significant potentials for lowering costs and optimizing processes, thus improving the conditions for a more efficient utilization of existing machinery and equipment. The chances to survive in price competition are not unfavorable; for instance, a steel corporation in Mexico took no more than a few years to develop into one of the world's lowest-cost producers.

Reorganization is followed by efforts aimed at developing more favorable locations for export-oriented firms (e.g. in the vicinity of a port), improving quality, and concentrating on products with especially good export chances. If a favorable economic policy climate is created, the consequence will be – as in the case of Chile – small and medium-sized firms geared to exporting from the very outset.

4. In countries that so far have only attained a low level of industrialization, firms must try to develop competitive advantages above all in resource-based and labor-intensive industries. When it turns its natural competitive advantages and lower wage costs to account, an exporting country is in a position to exploit an often significant specialization potential. The condition for maximizing the use of existing productive capacities and optimizing existing comparative advantages is that business organization, technology, and marketing be modernized:

– In the sectors of mining, agriculture, and raw-materials-based industries, the goal must be to achieve the international level of best practice. For some products, however, sharp competition in international markets – in particular in agriculture – not infrequently triggers declines in prices. Many DCs succeed in countering this tendency by rapidly diversifying the products they export, e.g. in agriculture or fishery (Jaffee 1993).

– Raw-materials-based industries (food-processing, textiles, footwear, furniture, and basic manufactured goods, above all hydrocarbon- and energy-intensive primary goods) may benefit in the short term from a significant latitude for modernization by utilizing low-priced raw-materials inputs, new organizational concepts, and state-of-the art technology. Furthermore, many food-processing or wood-working industries (furniture, printing and graphics) are accessible to intra-branch upgrading, and are thus able to break into areas of higher value added. Since basic manufactured goods require high capital inputs, joint ventures with foreign corporations are on the rise. Although production surpluses in the international markets often restrict the sales volume of these industries, an improvement of their medium-term prospects in connection with changes in the international division of labor is likely, since the ICs are expected to cut back on their production of many such products.

– In countries or regions characterized by especially underdeveloped industries, the first step toward international industrial division of labor is likely to be an intensification of labor-intensive assembly operations by foreign firms. There is room for the value-added share of such in-bond industries stemming from domestic production to rise significantly. In many cases, these firms even constitute the foundations on which foreign firms build up modern industrial subsidiaries in DCs. An additional field in which manufacturing competence counts is subcontracting by domestic firms to foreign firms, an element that can stimulate rapid growth of the technological competence of national private-sector firms.

– Following a protracted period of inward orientation, organization for export is of great importance. State-of-the-art telecommunications and database technologies should be used to improve marketing activities abroad. What is also important is the pooling of the products of small- and medium-sized firms for export, an area in which trading firms, large agro-industrial firms and export consortia of medium-sized firms are already making a contribution. Many DCs even succeed in joining marketing networks of advanced countries, e.g. China in Hong Kong and Taiwan. This enables them to boost their exports, in particular of relatively labor-intensive industrial goods, within a short time and rapidly diversify their export markets.

5. Following a period of economic reorientation, it is, even in many advanced countries, above all natural resources and resource-based industrial goods that contribute to exports. For Argentina, for example, the following was noted after a protracted period of industrial development: "... current specialization is based on technologically mature, capital-intensive, low value-added goods that require few specialized workers" (Bisang and Kosacoff 1993, 44). The market and world-market orientation of the firms in the technology-intensive industries of these countries entail particularly rigorous demands. When, in the short term, import policies are radically liberalized, many firms active in such industries (chemicals, machine-building, electronics, automobile industry, etc.) are forced out of business. In other cases, competition-oriented reorganization can lead to integration into the international division of labor, particularly if the firms involved supply parts and components. The local content is often sharply reduced as a means of making final assembly profitable.

The privatization of public-sector enterprises for the most part strengthens the group of national private major firms. Their size is also increased by mergers and take-overs of mid-size firms. Some major national firms employ highly qualified expert personnel and have a significant R&D potential. Their capital is for the most part adequate to enable them to rationalize dynamically and intensify their advertising efforts. When they introduce new concepts of organization, production, and marketing, they often succeed in swiftly boosting their international competitiveness. The condition for this is that they have access to a well-trained workforce. In advanced DCs with many years of inward-looking industrial orientation, the modernization of major domestic firms leads to a gradual integration into the international division of labor in a great variety of industries, in some cases even including high-tech sectors.

The responses of hitherto inward-looking subsidiaries of foreign industrial corporations to this reorientation in economic policy will

differ in many respects: some will leave; others will put off modernization in view of low levels of domestic demand, although it is these
firms that will come under growing pressure from imports. If domestic
demand proves interesting, firms' thinking about regional and
international strategies is also likely to prove positive. The most
important example of rapid modernization attended by pronounced
export orientation is Mexico's automobile industry. There, the NAFTA
perspective has also given rise to new final assembly plants geared to
the international level of best practice as well as the establishment of
suppliers in their proximity.

6. It is not at all rare for countries in the transitional phase to experience setbacks. This phase will vary in length depending on specific
conditions. In many countries it is especially difficult to put a new
macropolicy in place (for example Brazil; Meyer-Stamer 1995); others
are faced with a lack of dynamism at the microlevel (for example
Bolivia; Messner 1993). In many countries the development of the
mesolevel is neglected – in part owing to overconfidence in market
forces, in part because the state, itself undergoing reform, is unable to
participate in shaping the mesolevel. It often happens that reorientation
gains a foothold at the macrolevel and the microlevel, while the goal of
systematically improving competitiveness is accorded too little
attention.

1.2   Securing Endogenous and Nationally Controlled
         Development

The speed at which the competence of the key groups of actors in
controlling and stimulating the industrialization process and social
development grows tends to differ from country to country. Some of
the reasons for this, in particular sociocultural and intra- and international power-political factors, are difficult to grasp empirically. Six
important factors deserve to be underlined: overall strategy, the
definition of sequences, the development of sectors, the interlinkage of
domestic and foreign capabilities, financial-sector policy, and competition policy.

1. Development and implementation of a realistic overall strategy: The most important instrument of national control is an overall strategy keyed to a national consensus on a set of shared values and medium- and long-term goals, the mobilization of endogenous development potentials, involving in particular a strengthening of the national private-sector, a utilization of external experience and potentials, and the reduction of any external disruptive factors that may strongly impede, or even render impossible, internal processes of learning and development. This strategy is sustained by a interlinkage of national forces based on a cooperative relationship between government and strategic groups. The core of the dialogue is made up by coordination of and agreement on individual policies, in particular the mesolevel, achieved with the aim of jointly strengthening the competitiveness of the national economy.

The first task is to break out of the traditional circulus vitiosus of a sterile short-sightedness *(cortoplazismo)* by laying the groundwork for a joint medium- and long-term vision defining the direction which industrialization and social development is to be given. The next step is to establish a pattern of organization geared to national consensus and interlinkage, one that makes it possible to lower costs and to organize for export within the framework of a competition-oriented indus-trialization. Government has the tasks of supporting the process of systemic reorganization of the national private sector, wherever this should become necessary, and, as reorganization progresses, to stimulate a dynamic and broad-based learning process in the various sectors of society. Important instruments to this end include active and selective educational, research, financial, technology, and industrial policies that lend themselves to building an industrial system.

The overall strategy is borne by a national network of forces based on cooperative relations between a lean government and the other strategic groups. Dialogue centers on coordinating individual policies with an eye to strengthening, through joint efforts, the competitiveness of the national economy (see Box 2).

Box 2:
Elements of a comprehensive conceptualization of world market oriented technological and industrial development

1. Concept of endogenous development: every society must, on its own account, come to terms with technology and its consequences, i.e. recognize its own development reserves and fully utilize its existing latent development potentials. The conditions for this are national integration and a national consensus on the direction in which social development is to proceed.

2. Concept of national control: The most important groups of actors (government, industry, intermediary organizations) come to terms on a realistic overall strategy and modify it along the lines of the requirement profile of the economy. This strategy is aimed at an industrialization process shaped by a strong government and a strong economy and by cooperative forms of action on the part of the central actors.

3. Concept of efficient allocation of resources: The task is not chiefly to seek to identify and close "capital gaps", but instead to undertake efforts to enhance the efficiency of capital utilization, the average productivity, and the average rate of return of the economy. As a rule, it is possible to mobilize sufficient funding for profitable projects. Productivity-driven growth and world-market-oriented competition have proven able to ensure increased efficiency of the utilization of national resources (labor, material, energy, capital), which is of the utmost significance in ecological terms.

4. Concept of strengthening strong market forces: Relatively autonomous government creates functioning markets via its regulatory activities, promotes the formation of structures, provides incentives for the private sector (e.g. by encouraging SMEs) and contributes toward expanding their room for external maneuver. By reinforcing perceptible business initiative and entrepreneurial strengths (picking the winners), government of this sort proceeds selectively, i.e. not indiscriminately, and sets store on demonstration effects.

5. Concept of innovation- and export-oriented networking: The direction taken jointly by the groups of actors is reinforced through interlinkage mechanisms
–   between workforce and management at the firm level
–   among the firms themselves,
–   between industrial associations and trade unions,
–   between industry and private and public R&D, and municipal and regional administration,
–   between industry, state, research, and intermediary organizations.

Networks bringing together the relevant actors, e.g. inter-firm production and innovation networks or networks devised to gather and process information and facilitate the joint (cooperative) decision-making processes of strategic groups, can effectively supplement or, in given cases, correct the role of the market, i.e.

Box 2 (continued)

its competitive functions. Networks can also be used to gear a society not only to the exigencies of a competitive economy but also to a socially and ecologically compatible strategy of qualitative growth.

6. Concept of full utilization of existing and development of new specialization opportunities: The growth industries of the international economy and international trade consist not only of technology-intensive segments, they also include labor- and capital-intensive segments (e.g. toys, sporting goods, clothing, furniture) which also offer specialization chances for DCs that are just beginning with industrial development. What is important is to examine existing fields of specialization, single out the most promising of them for further development, concentrate additional resources in a limited number of new fields of specialization, and to do so with an eye to existing or potential supply strengths, while not losing sight of market dynamics and the strategies of competitor countries.

7. Concept of optimization of supply-side strength: The supply conditions available to an economy are developed by utilizing advantages associated with learning, interfacing, and interlinkage. The core element is national technological capability – the capacity to develop a clear grasp of the technologies available, to assess and select the right technology, to adapt and improve the technology, and, finally, to develop technologies – as the most important presupposition for international competitiveness and socioeconomic development. The effectiveness and intensity of technology transfer depend on technological competence at firm and government level.

8. Concept of the full and optimal utilization of domestic, regional, and international market demand: The demand conditions with which an economy is faced are enhanced by exploiting the potential offered by the domestic, regional, and international market. Enlarging the dimension of the market via free-trade zones, expanded to form customs unions, so as to heighten the investment interest of domestic and external firms is of particular importance in the initial phase of industrialization. It is furthermore important to diversify markets geographically. What counts over the medium term is a rapid expansion of domestic demand, since this provides a solid base for major segments of an economy.

9. Concept of high-profile players: As the strength of national groups of actors grows, external conditions can likewise be improved. Players gain influence on changes in the international industrial division of labor as soon as they begin to seek "cooperation and competition" with foreign firms and, from the very start, make use of their marketing organizations. There are signs that indicate that in the 1990s more and more DCs are vigorously resisting growing protectionism on the part of groups of ICs. Joining regional IC trade or integration groups, or an open, constructive regionalism among the DCs themselves enhance the conditions for an active integration into the international economy.

2. Definition of priorities and sequences: The transitional phase entails above all the risk of sticking too long with low value-added export products, but there is also a risk of attempting, without being in possession of the wherewithal required, to advance into the sphere dominated by technology-intensive industries. Managing a step-by-step approach requires, both of the state and of the business sector, high levels of competence in setting priorities in keeping with international demands and existing national conditions. It also calls for the strategy selected to be modified, if necessary, in such a way as to bring it into line with the requirements and goals of a new sequence.

In the first sequence following reorientation, that is in the initial transition, it is at least possible to create the conditions necessary to advance into a second sequence. This will be the case when government is at pains to harness and to expand the strengths developed at all four system levels and to interlink the levels. Government will also, where necessary, continue to develop its macropolicy and foster among the different groups of actors a shared vision keyed to the new frame of reference. And it will also concentrate – likewise in close cooperation with industry – on developing mesopolicies and mesolevel institutions.

In the second sequence industry advances into fields of higher-level specialization. Its needs for qualified manpower with technological know-how and its demand for R&D services will grow. New organizational and marketing concepts should gain currency in a growing number of firms. It is then, especially in the modern centers of industrial conglomeration, that national advantages will begin to look interesting for innovative foreign industries as well. The capital market is becoming integrated in this sequence.

It is not seldom, especially after a long phase of import substitution, that firms from a variety of industries that have been stepping up their export activities will begin to occupy "niches". But it is also important for such firms to join forces in marching within the sectors as a means of boosting innovative dynamism and competitive strength in a functional and spatial network, e.g. in world-market-specialized clusters (industrial complexes or industrial districts). It is also important to build up new industrial clusters, with government and the business sector jointly defining the priority sectors and the approach to be taken in successively increasing the number of such clusters.

The most important features encountered toward the onset of the second sequence are a successful integration of the national economy – based on the international best-practice organization of production – into the international competition for locations, growth, and exports and a high level of strategic capability on the part of the central groups of actors, including intensive national networking efforts.

This can make it possible to advance into the third sequence, i.e. into broad-based industrialization geared to "catching up", even in high-tech industries. To be sure, the development of high-tech industries requiring the allocation of substantial resources for R&D is so difficult that not many countries are apt to succeed in it.

The demands placed on government and the business sector, and what the latter expects of the mesolevel, grow from sequence to sequence. This was especially clear in the countries of East Asia: world-market-oriented industrialization was conceived strategically there; the actors sought success in a joint dynamic learning process and concentrated on a limited number of fields of specialization. Selective policies (specific support for individual industries, corporate groups, and technologies and selective export promotion and import protection) were used to strengthen industry's international competitiveness and foster productivity- and technology-driven growth.

3. **Policies and institutions of sectoral development**: At the outset, the greater part of the industrial goods exported consists of technologically mature products with low value added. There is a lack of specialized manpower. Following a protracted period of industrial import substitution, there are, however – in contrast to earlier processes of world-market-oriented industrialization – exports of technology-intensive industrial goods (e.g. automotive parts and components, electrotechnical and electronic equipment). The prime consideration is to enable existing industries to boost their productivity.

What frequently proves important to progressing on a broad front from resource-based and labor-intensive industries to capital- and skill-intensive industries is a limited period of trade protection tailored to safeguarding the industrial learning process and serving to lower costs and achieve viability.

Policies and institutions of sectoral development which – as in East and Southeast Asia – elaborate strategies aimed at areas of specialization, concentrating forces and proceeding step by step, and geared to providing firms with information and credit can distinctly reduce the period of time for which trade protection is required. Demonstration effects on the part of highly competitive SMEs can give rise to a pronounced imitative potential.

Sectoral development institutions can take the lead in pointing the way to and supporting structural development at the firm level: in many industries (e.g. textiles), 4-5 major and 15-20 mid-size core firms will account for the greater part of exports. Programs designed to reorganize and develop production chains are more apt to strengthen international competitiveness than isolated SME promotion measures. A competition-oriented process of cluster-building (SMEs, including clusters of small firms) can contribute to export growth (e.g. in the shoe industry) if the process is supported over a limited period of time. Industry, design, and technology institutes are likewise a source of encouragement for competition-oriented modernization of groups of firms. This also applies for technology and marketing programs, initial support for national trading firms, and incentives to the formation of local and regional networks. Overcoming problems related to organization and communication is one way of lowering costs. When vocational training programs of R&D institutions are to be expanded, focusing on industries already strong in exporting can accelerate learning processes at the firm level.

4. **Combining domestic and foreign capabilities**: Economic policy – and this is crucial – is formulated and implemented in the national interest. Direct foreign investment is, as far as possible, integrated in such way as to intensify existing national dynamics. Specific needs for

support should be articulated concretely to donor countries. What is important at the levels of both business and government is to harness foreign capabilities for learning processes that make it possible to work out specific profiles of their own.

The recommendations of multilateral institutions are heeded as long as they can be brought in line with national objectives. This is true in particular for any specific relationship between market and state. "Selectivity" implies that physical infrastructure and the institutions involved in forming human capital are developed in keeping with specific national potentials and the needs of industry.

5. **Financial-sector policy**: Capital-market liberalization not infrequently jeopardizes the financial sector's orientation toward the requirements of the productive sector. The reasons for this include high interest rates (in connection with anti-inflation policy), the short terms for which credit is granted, and security requirements that can be met only by major firms. Heavy short-term capital inflows could endanger a country's future competitiveness. To the extent that they consist of speculative capital, high portfolio investments should be fended off, whereas direct foreign investment ought to be encouraged. Reliable and competitive real exchange-rate levels and interest rates declining in real terms heighten investment interest and the security firms need for their planning.

Private pension funds can constitute important instruments for stimulating the capital market and, in tendency, increasing the savings rate and levels of long-term lending. The viability of such funds requires government supervision to ensure that legally binding, risk-limiting guidelines are met in investing the funds and that mismanagement due to corruption is ruled out. Given attractive investment opportunities, taxes on luxury and leisure articles (as, e.g., in Taiwan), aimed against extravagant lifestyles, can provide a contribution to raising savings rates and increasing the volume of investment.

6. **Competition policy**: Average company size (in Latin America roughly 1/10 of the IC firms in equivalent industrial segments; Katz

1993) is an obstacle to industrial mass production as well as to any R&D conducive to building up competitive positions in the high-tech sector. On the other hand, in the ICs transnational corporations, including interlocked major corporations, continue to grow in importance. Not only are they competitors in the world market, they are also competitors in the areas of imports and manufacturing in the DCs themselves. Furthermore, the expansion of small firms to be observed in ICs proceeds as a rule in symbiotic relation to major industry. If the manufacturing techniques of major firms are restricted, the – complementary – dynamics of the fields in which small firms are active will also tend to diminish. This is the core problem facing SME development in industrially underdeveloped countries.

One important basic decision governing market structures consists of safeguarding the self-regulating function of market processes via framework conditions laid down by government (framework of competition policy), while at the same time taking measures to improve competitive conditions. Aside from reducing positions of market domination, safeguarding competition in domestic markets, and setting up obstacles to dumping imports, what is called for is a strengthening of national private-sector competitive potentials so as to improve the chances of domestic industry against strongly competitive direct investors and import competitors.

This will give rise to countervailing market power and a potential for successful cooperation with foreign corporations. Once an adequate number of independent firms are active in the various markets, i.e. as soon as competition is able to fulfill its overall economic incentive and control function, it is – in view of the great demands placed by the world market – possible to tolerate export oligopolies.

2   Managing the Transition – the Main Tasks

2.1   Rebalancing the Public and the Private Sector

Any strategy which focuses on developing the productive forces of a
national economy and is at the same time geared to the world market as
its frame of reference requires a far-reaching and thorough redefinition
of the relationship between the public and private sectors. This requires
the initiation of a process that strengthens market forces and increases
the latitudes available to develop private initiative. This process above
all entails examining the role of the public sector as a supplier of goods
and services. This is true for the supply of private goods in competitive
markets, the supply of public goods, and industries in which competition is restricted by a natural monopoly.

1. **Withdrawal of the public sector from competitive markets**: As a
supplier of goods and services, the public sector should withdraw from
markets in which, in principle, the conditions of functioning competition can be created. For the following reasons in particular, efficiency
gains may be expected from the privatization of public-sector enterprises:

–   Interference of government authorities and agencies in entre-
     preneurial decision-making processes will decrease.

–   There exist stronger incentives to raise efficiency in production
     and the quality of products when the returns can be appropriated
     privately.

–   The trade in business shares and business themselves in the capital
     markets leads to continuous ratings of managerial decisions and a
     higher level of pressure to achieve success than is the case for
     public-sector enterprises

–   Private firms are generally subject to more pressure to operate
     efficiently than publicly owned firms, since, when state-owned
     firms incur losses, the public sector is obliged to pick up the tab in
     order to ensure their survival.

Privatization of state-owned enterprises will, however, lead to higher efficiency in production and allocation only they are actually faced with heightened competitive pressures. Privatization must therefore be accompanied by market deregulation. This includes in particular the successive dismantling of any exaggerated import protection, administrative barriers to market access, and price controls.

2. Privatization of the supply of public goods and natural monopolies: Since the 1980s privatization in ICs and DCs has also included areas that have traditionally been seen as classical tasks of government. This goes above all for segments of telecommunications, power and energy supply, and the transport sector. Initial experiences indicate that efficiency gains can be made by shifting the interface between private and public economic activities. Such gains can, for instance, be realized when government is restricted to running the networks and leaves the sectors to be structural competitively, e.g. electricity generation, telecommunications terminal equipment, and value-added services, to private suppliers. In many ICs and DCs, even distribution networks covered by a natural monopoly have been privatized. In this case, careful regulation of prices and supply are required to realize efficiency gains.

Higher efficiency in the provision of public goods and goods subject to a natural monopoly can also be achieved by granting franchises and contracting out service activities. It is in this way possible to create competition for markets in which there is no competition. Such approaches have proven efficient only when, on the one hand, the services provided by private suppliers are carefully defined and supervised and, on the other hand, competition among suppliers is not subject to any sharp restraints (e.g. sunk costs). There are examples of success in the fields of public transport, construction and maintenance of roads, bridges and port facilities, and public waste disposal systems. All in all, the success of privatization of the supply of public goods and of natural monopolies is heavily dependent on the effectiveness of government regulation.

3. Core elements of a comprehensive privatization strategy: Any redefinition of the relationship between the public and private sectors thus involves much more than the quickest possible conversion of public property into private property. Privatization of state-owned enterprises is a politically sensitive process. Any privatization strategy that arbitrarily picks out individual enterprises or sectors will soon meet defeat at the hands of public resistance. Government must instead show itself resolved to put the whole of the public sector to the test and develop a comprehensive privatization strategy. The core elements of a privatization strategy of this type include the following steps:

– Selection of the enterprises to be privatized: Aside from the basic decision as to which central public tasks are to remain with government and which should be privatized, it is necessary to select the enterprises that are to be privatized over the short and medium term. This involves setting priorities. Rapid privatization is recommendable for firms relatively small both as regards their operating capital and their product markets. These firms can be privatized via a competitive bidding process, without any extensive regulation. The larger the firm, the greater the efforts required to prepare the privatization process. Suppliers of public goods as well as natural monopolies can be privatized only after a regulatory framework has been developed.

– Development of marketable enterprises: Numerous state-owned enterprises in ICs and DCs are incapable of being privatized because of their size, their line of products and services, and their poor financial records. In many cases, enterprises will have to be deconcentrated, freed of debt, and rehabilitated before they can be privatized. How far government should go here is a controversial question. But a good deal of experience has been made with situations in which the competitiveness and profitability of public-sector enterprises was achieved through government rehabilitation efforts. But as a rule this process presupposes changes both managerial and institutional, namely bringing in new management on the basis of a management contracts to supervise the rehabilitation programs. Enterprises no longer accessible to privatization and rehabilitation will have to be liquidated.

−   Determination of the market value of enterprises: The value of
    major state-owned enterprises must be established in a thorough
    corporate audit, which will as a rule be conducted by experienced
    international consultants. The prices of smaller enterprises can be
    determined by a competitive process in the market. But here too
    government will have to set a minimum price.

−   Choice of a privatization procedure: There are many ways to
    privatize enterprises; they extend from informal negotiations with
    one or more bidders, standardized auction procedures, to the pri-
    vatization of company shares on a stock exchange. All of these
    procedures have their advantages and disadvantages. What speaks
    in favor of privatization via informal sales procedures is that this
    approach permits discussions on prices and the business concept
    involved and enables the sellers to inform themselves as to the
    bidder's competence. The buyer's entrepreneurial competence is a
    factor of crucial importance to the success of any privatization. In
    particular when major enterprises are privatized, it is important not
    simply to favor the prospective buyer who offers the highest price,
    but to choose the bidder who advances the most convincing busi-
    ness concept. The disadvantage of informal sales negotiations is
    their low level of transparency and the comparatively high level of
    effort and expense required by the negotiation process. Such ne-
    gotiations demand a competent and reliable government authority
    able to transact the privatization. Informal negotiated solutions are
    above all the best approach to privatizing medium- and large-size
    enterprises. The advantage of standardized auction procedures is
    that it is in this way comparatively simple to determine a sales
    price via bidder competition. Sale by auction does, however, rely
    on competition among prospective buyers, and this procedure is
    thus best suited for SMEs. Privatization via the stock exchange is
    the most demanding approach. This requires a developed capital
    market; the firm to be privatized will have to be profitable, and the
    transaction will require comprehensive evaluation and control
    procedures. This privatization procedure is thus suited only to
    larger enterprises. Regardless of the privatization procedure se-
    lected, participation of a foreign investor with proven sectoral

know-how in the new firm can markedly increase the chances of achieving sustained gains in efficiency. Restraints on competition for foreign bidders lower the returns stemming from privatization and may even impair the efficiency of the privatized firm.

– Accompanying measures for newly privatized enterprises: If the privatized firm is a supplier of public goods or a holder of a natural monopoly, the government will have to provide for accompanying measures such as regulation of supply and price formation. Other privatized enterprises will also often require accompanying measures regarding complex privatization agreements, deferment of payment, assumption of government liability obligations, rehabilitation subsidies, and the like.

2.2   Assessing the Potential of Domestic Industries to Adjust and Restructure

In the phase of inward orientation, many DCs developed an overdiversified industrial structure. The recommendation that such countries develop a specialization profile implies that some firms, and even industries, will have to go.

An evaluation of existing industry determines which firms or industries are closer to the internationally prevalent level of efficiency than others and are thus in a more favorable starting position. Preparations should include independent evaluations of the efficiency and technological competence of sectors and individual firms, conducted by international industry experts of high repute. Aside from traditional methods of cost comparison, instruments such as benchmarking should be employed, i.e. the analysis of data which define the relative efficiency level of one firm as compared with others (e.g. warehousing, value-added shares of through-put times, amount of rework, rejects, and scrap).

Assessment is especially difficult with key industries, in particular the capital goods industry, which may have required considerable effort to build up under import substitution. This process saw the emergence of firms that sharply reflect the weaknesses of an exaggeratedly inward-looking industry – inefficient production, lack of technological dynamics, overdiversification. A process of consolidation via mergers and closures of factories in such industries will prove inevitable in the course of transition. At the same time there is a great danger that valuable technological know-how (above all manufacturing technology) acquired at considerable expense may be lost. It is therefore especially important to implement selective policies designed to prevent any overly far-reaching adjustment process.

Industrial modernization policy should aim at structuring the capital goods industry in such a way as to tailor it to the projected specialization profile of the national economy.

The conversion of armaments plants is extremely complex (and seldom successful). Armaments manufacturers are faced with severe problems in surviving in competitive markets, especially technology-intensive civilian markets. The gap between the innovation cycles of civilian and military products continues to grow (at the expense of military products). Furthermore, civilian markets differ in their requirements from military markets – e.g. user-friendliness as opposed to resistance to extreme environmental conditions. Armaments firms find it particularly difficult to adapt organization and technology to these new requirements. They therefore have little to contribute during the transition to a competition-oriented economy.

2.3   Targeting Priority Sectors

The transition from an inward-looking to a world-market orientation calls for development of economic and structural policies keyed to the adaptability and responsiveness of firms so as to avoid any excessive adjustment processes and support any tenable specialization profile advanced by industry. The experiences available indicate that the task of rapidly opening their markets to foreign trade often overburdens DCs, especially since they seldom have access to an efficient industrial environment and are often faced with non-functioning internal markets.

The process of transition should entail developing, as rapidly as possible, a number of internationally competitive clusters. Selective mesopolicies focused on priority sectors can contribute to bringing firms or groups of firms capable of development up to international efficiency levels. Only in priority sectors will it be possible to build up properly structured mesolevel, i.e. vocational schools, technology institutions, and information systems. The necessity to develop specialization patterns meets with a scarcity of financial and manpower resources. In addition, selective trade policies can create the time frame required to build up competitive advantages and to advance the restructuring process at the entrepreneurial and sectoral levels.

Generally speaking, it is possible to distinguish three targeting variants:

−   As a result of the altered economic framework conditions, new export-oriented fields of specialization are developed in the process of change (e.g. Chile: exports of fruit, fish, timber); their commercial environment should be developed systematically with an eye to facilitating the difficult search and learning processes with which firms are faced. In this case, mesopolicies can follow up on market selection processes.

−   Based on an assessment of the potential of domestic industries to adjust and restructure (through evaluation, identification of efficient sectors), an attempt should be made to "strengthen the strong". If this is neglected, the process of rapid liberalization and opening up to foreign trade can lead to the destruction of even potentially modernizable segments with a high development potential. "Non-discrimination" between objectively obsolete industries and modern industries entailing a lack of flanking policies to support the latter is expensive in both economic and social terms. Research on Poland has shown that here rapid trade liberalization has led to the collapse industries which were entirely competitive as far as their production structures were concerned. In spite of sufficient competence in manufacturing, these industries failed to penetrate Western markets immediately following the rapid collapse of their traditional markets within COMECON. Export credits and other active export promotion measures would have been able to ensure the survival of these industries (Brunner 1993). Such forms of destruction of productive capital should if at all possible be prevented via assessing, targeting, and selective mesopolicies.

–   The most demanding task is the search for future economic fields in industries with a high value-added potential and development of an anticipatory structural policy. This form of targeting promises success only in connection with economic consolidation and on the basis of experience made in dialogue between firms, government, and science.

Targeting and selective mesopolicies are closely linked with the development of a complex monitoring system. What is essential in the initial phase is a strategic outlook on the part of government institutions (ministry of economics, advisory groups) as regards targeting. Business associations and lobbies will primarily represent particular interests and push to define their own industries as strategic centers. This phase of transition will be marked by activities of strategically oriented actors in public institutions, with independent consultants and experts aiming at localizing industrial cores with development potential. The second phase of economic consolidation and successive expansion of the industrial base will be geared to developing a more broadly structured monitoring system based on a pluralism of actors and institutions. Economic research institutes, university-level research institutions, sector-specific technology and consulting institutions, industrial associations and private-sector research institutions, trade unions, and consulting services contribute to continuously improving the information base on the dynamics in the productive sector. These institutions interact via the publication of studies and exchange of conflicting scientific opinions, congresses, cooperative research.

The know-how accumulated in the institutions and the formal and informal forms of interaction between the institutions (interlinkage) are conducive to a continuous learning process on the part of all actors as regards economic and industrial location policy, increase transparency as regards the strengths, weaknesses, and challenges with which industry must contend, and improve the ability of firms and private- and public-sector institutions to define an orientation of their own. While many DCs are initially concerned with creating the institutions in which know-how on the productive sector can be accumulated (type: Economic Planning Board/Republic of Korea), the accumulation of such know-how is largely a self-propelling process in advanced countries: for the institutions mentioned communicate via the exchange of studies, seminars, joint research projects, advisory boards, and the like. Aside from this horizontal self-organization, focal points of research policy are as a rule set by research promotion institutions (type: *Deutsche Forschungsgemeinschaft* / German Research Council).

But translating this know-how into economic policy is a strategic decision. Government institutions in the areas of economic and industrial-location policy here again have the important task of coordinating and focusing the existing know-how, illuminating development corridors, formulating, in cooperation with strategic actors, medium-range visions, and on this basis shaping the most optimal locational structures possible. These "soft forms of governance" differ clearly from traditional planning concepts in terms of their interactive and procedural character.

Aside from the selective improvement of supply conditions, it is also necessary to take into account the demand potentials and conditions governing market access in the specific sectors of the international economy in the course of the process of targeting priority sectors. For DCs, it is especially important here to realize that the growth sectors of international industry and trade include not only the technology-intensive sectors but also other segments in which industrially less advanced DCs have specialization chances (eg textiles and garments, wood products, fruit and vegetables).

2.4   Removing the Anti-Export Bias and Controlling the Speed of Import Liberalization

Instead of strengthening a national economy, long-term protectionism causes higher costs for consumers as well as a growing level of inefficiency, a process that ends in declining industrialization dynamics. If the political leadership groups are too weak to sustain a gradual import liberalization, protection will be diminished by a shock effect. In any case, import protection should be reduced tangibly over the short and medium term in many industries so as to generate adjustment pressure on as many firms as possible. The anti-export bias should be eliminated and replaced with an export-biased trade regime. It will also often prove necessary to remove export incentives that burden the government budget; the task always includes a rationalization of trade-policy incentives. At a lower level of import protection, i.e. a high level of import competition and attendant pressure to export, the world market becomes the economy's frame of reference. The pressure in the direction of reorientation and restructuring should, however, not be allowed to overburden the adjustment capacity of an economy, 95 % and more of which may consist of SMEs. Under conditions of quasi free trade (e.g. import tariffs of 10 % and low NTBs), many firms capable of specialization are forced to quit when faced with competition from experienced major foreign corporations. Accordingly, if more and more market segments are opened to import competition, trade-balance deficits will grow, strongly impairing not only the national private sector's adjustment potential but also its development potential.

Resource-based and labor-intensive industries require little protection. The subsidiaries of foreign corporations need at best a brief period of import protection. But the path of national private-sector capital- and skill-intensive industries to international competitiveness is a stony one. They are forced to compete with foreign corporations with large, sometimes even protected, domestic and regional markets and with superior technological competence. One factor of crucial significance in providing domestic industries with latitude for development is managing the delicate relationship between the level of import protection and the economy's competitive strength. Development protection is often required only for a limited period if it is accompanied by complementary promotional measures. Without any such selective import protection (timetable for learning and shaping competitive advantages), balanced in terms of competitive and development potentials, dynamic industrial development finds itself up against nearly insurmountable obstacles. When such protection is in place and, as soon as new concepts of industrial organization have been introduced following the difficult phase of transition and consolidation, DCs are entirely in a position to achieve in the medium term levels of efficiency and quality that may even exceed those in ICs.

It is particularly difficult to build up technology-intensive industries and to integrate priority sectors of this type in the technological race between competitively strong countries. The pragmatic policy of liberalization and protection (selective integration strategy) pursued in East Asia was in this case largely based on formal and informal mechanisms for protecting the domestic market and strengthening the national technological base:

– via tariff-like levies, quantitative import restrictions, import licenses, consultation procedures involving the industries concerned, and programs aimed at strengthening domestic suppliers, and

– specific mechanisms such as restricted access for foreign firms to national marketing channels and directed credits for domestic institutions.

Today, both these mechanisms and a policy of direct and indirect export encouragement, e.g. via preferential credits, are the preferred approaches.

As industrialization progresses, and in close connection with the achieved levels of competitiveness, domestic import protection can be reduced, always with an eye to a cautious liberalization perspective, in part on the basis of a medium-term liberalization timetable and precise monitoring of import development. Persistently high NTBs are used to avoid excessive adjustment frictions and balance-of-trade deficits. In Japan or the Republic of Korea, the indirect restrictions on access to markets continue to be high – even in view of a "rapid shift in industrial structure toward capital- and knowledge-intensive industries" (World Bank 1993, 274).

2.5   Setting Priorities in Techno-Industrial Infrastructure Development

Advanced developing countries: One urgent task facing the advanced DCs is to build up a national system of innovation. This presupposes the establishment of priorities in the R&D sector, a reorganization of the system of science, and stimulation of technological networks.

1. R&D: In advanced DCs, setting priorities in the field of R&D is first of all a political-organizational problem. There are frequently diverse actors in this field whose activities are in the best case uncoordinated, in the worst case directed against one another. One approach to overcoming disarticulation and the lack of a strategy is offered by national technology dialogues. In them, representatives of government administration are brought together with entrepreneurs and bankers, scientists and engineers, and representatives of key groups of society. These dialogues are utilized to identify the most important bottlenecks and to formulate action-oriented approaches.

2. Systems of science: In many advanced DCs, there exists a comparatively developed structure of universities and research institutions. But they are frequently faced with three problems:

– Their financial endowment is inadequate, which makes it difficult for them to retain qualified scientists and engineers; or these persons are required to employ a larger share of their working time on activities apart from their actual tasks.

– They are too extensively bureaucratized, their institutional flexibility is inadequate.

– They are geared primarily to basic research and engage in very little applications-oriented research tailored to the needs of domestic industry; they have too little contact to the private-sector.

The priority task is therefore reorganization, rehabilitation, and reorientation, if not, indeed, closure and re-establishment of universities and research institutions. Funding should be keyed more to performance – their output of students and the funds they acquire for research and consulting services. At the same time, care must be taken that the revenues from research and consulting services directly benefit the departments and facilities involved, and not simply their administration. It is in this way possible to stimulate cooperation with the private sector and provide disincentives to any tendencies toward brain drain.

3. Universities: One further important aspect is the setting of priorities in the reorganization and/or construction of universities. The traditional model was the universal university which offered all fields of study. If universities are to make a contribution to modernizing industry, the appropriate approach would be to strengthen the departments of sciences and engineering and to design them from the very outset with an eye to an applications orientation. Moreover, it is important to build up technical colleges beside traditional, scientifically oriented universities, which – on the successful German model – train engineers for practical tasks in close contact with industry. In both areas, universities and technical colleges, it is necessary to establish fields of specialization in the subjects in which a country wishes to strengthen and dynamize its base of advantages.

4. Technology institutions and technological networks: The attitudes of businessmen in DCs toward any close cooperation with institutions (and state-run ones, into the bargain) and other entrepreneurs extend for the most part from skepticism to rejection. What is behind these attitudes is fear of losing know-how to "copy-cats" and a pronounced competitive consciousness. Enterprises will only build networks when their benefits clearly exceed their costs and, in addition, the socio-cultural conditions, in particular with regard to a basis for trust, are

favorable. Any construction or restructuring of technology institutions and development of technological networks is therefore an extremely demanding task. Taking the following aspects into account can help to diminish the likelihood of failure:

– Experience has shown that the success of R&D institutions correlates closely with their degree of specialization: institutions with a clear-cut mandate and a clearly defined orientation, e.g. in terms of a given branch of industry, tend more to entertain close contacts with users and to generate results that are implemented. It is for this reason that in particular specialized R&D institutions (e.g. wood-working, metallurgy, food-processing, textiles and clothing) should be encouraged. Institutions of this type can also develop competence in surveying the technology on offer throughout the world and stimulate the transfer of technology from abroad. Technology transfer agencies covering the entire spectrum of industrial technology, on the other hand, have proven less effective in the past.

– Government or parastatal R&D institutions should operate with the clear objective of maintaining close contact with possible users. The funds they are allocated could be made conditional on proof of such cooperation. Users with sufficient financial power should contribute to the financing of such institutions. It must, however, be borne in mind that the willingness of user firms to pay is low when the investment is for joint R&D projects, i.e. investment with a relatively long pay-back period; this applies above all for SMEs. Enterprises are more willing to pay when the institution can contribute directly to solving acute problems (e.g. specific weak points in production processes, quality problems, repair of defective machines). This form of direct help can serve as a "Trojan horse" for any long-term technology consulting service

– As far as SMEs are concerned, it will often also prove necessary to seek to establish contact with them via technology extension services and encourage and support their processes of technological modernization; for these firms for the most part display a low level of knowledge on new equipment and organizational techniques and often lack sufficient awareness of the problems involved in systematic innovation efforts.

– In recent years, quality programs have proven to be a promising approach, e.g. linked with the attempt to meet the ISO 9000 standard. Such programs are not isolated activities, they are, rather, conditioned on a reorganization of a firm's entire value chain. This implies introducing new technological hardware no less than implementing new management concepts. Technology institutions with the right know-how (that they in turn acquire, e.g., via internal quality programs) can provide important support here. They can organize seminars, but also provide consulting services for individual firms. Quality programs are thus a point of departure for the building up of industrial technology extension services.

– In many advanced DCs, the model of promoting the establishment of technology-oriented firms via the provision of facilities (incubators) and management consulting has proven successful. The aim here is in particular to support an incipient exchange of experience and information between the users of incubators.

5. Information infrastructure: A private information acquisition system, set up with government support, can broaden the available database on products, markets, competitors, technical procedures, and patents. This makes it possible to reduce information deficits that can cause high costs. The task is to avoid faulty investment decisions, to reduce any duplication of R&D and superfluous patent applications, and to focus information on regional and international markets. A market information instrument of this type enhances market transparency, thus improving the chances of market-oriented management and access to markets and familiarizing firms with techniques of researching information in databases. On-line research reduces company costs. Information markets at the same time improve the conditions for dialogue, early identification of technological trends, and selective technology and industrial policies.

6. MSTQ: One important flanking control instrument of national industrial policy is a system of measuring, standards, testing, and qual-

ity assurance (MSTQ). At the outset, reaching a decision in favor of one of the various standards systems offered by competing industrial countries is of considerable importance. At the international level, the costs for the manufacture of semi-finished and finished goods rise because components are often not compatible, which increases the problems involved in maintaining and operating technical equipment. This problem will decline in significance as ISO standards gain in currency.

For any industry geared to internationally valid rules, an integrated MSTQ system is an essential infrastructural investment. Often, only individual components of MSTQ are in use, which, in additional, are not keyed to one another. The task is therefore to integrate MSTQ within a national economy and, in particular, to encourage its systematic relation to industry, e.g. intensive consideration of company know-how in formulating quality programs or laying down industrial standards. What is also crucial to standardization is that the publications of international bodies (above all the ISO) be systematically followed and that in the medium term national organizations participate in its committees.

7. Conversion: Some countries are faced with the special problem that – isolated from the civilian sector – powerful high-tech islands have emerged there in the military and aerospace sector. They contribute little to civilian industrial development, although they do make claim to a major share of the available financial resources and scientific and engineering potential. It is urgent to effect a shift in favor of the civilian sector. Yet this tends not only to encounter political resistance, it also raises practical problems; for the conversion of a military research institution is no less complex than the conversion of an armaments plant. It is thus unlikely that conversion will lead to any technological push for the civilian sector.

Least developed countries (LDCs): The scientific-technical infrastructure of least developed countries is for the most part far from state-of-the-art. Building such infrastructure in these countries is a priority task for international development cooperation.

In LDCs, the need for technology institutions that operate their own R&D programs and transfer their innovations to the business sector is as a rule slight. The manufacturing sector is for the most part technologically underdeveloped and in need of ad hoc consulting services. But here the business sector lacks the receptive structures required for long-term technological projects carried out in cooperation with a technology institution.

Ad hoc technological consulting services should be guided by the existing training institutions which are in contact with firms or intend to establish such contact. It is, however, important to bear in mind here that the distrust of such institutions (particularly universities and independent institutions) among private firms is often considerable. "Confidence-building measures" are thus a crucial condition for the success of such projects.

Consulting services going above and beyond this can be provided by industry-specific institutions which should be capable of a scanning process extending beyond national borders. Many elements required to upgrade industrial firms in LDCs are available throughout the world – be it as mature industrial technology from ICs and advanced DCs, be in the form of medium-level or intermediate technology ("appropriate technology").

3   Capability Creation and Enhancement at the Microlevel: the Firms' Responsibilities

Industrial competitiveness emerges at the firm level. Ideally, all stages of the value chain are organized efficiently and effectively: research and product development, the linkage of product development and production, procurement and materials management, quality assurance, production, sales, and after-sales service.

Companies that emerged in closed economies are for the most part faced with deficiencies in each of these functional areas. Research and product development were of little significance, the goal being to imitate standardized products. Procurement and materials management were as disorganized as production because there was a lack of pressure to operate efficiently. Quality assurance had no priority because products of lower quality were marketable. It was often unnecessary to invest much effort in marketing because the products sold. And after-sales service, finally, was non-existent because there were hardly any competitors to whom frustrated customers could switch.

Moreover, firms emerged in many DCs during the phase of inward orientation that went too far in their diversification efforts as a result of the narrowness of the domestic market. Under new, competition-oriented framework conditions, these firms must strive to identify core competences and develop a clear-cut specialization profile. This is the condition necessary for them to approach the minimum efficient plant size.

The transition to a competitive orientation has seen firms faced with the challenge of having, largely, to reorganize the entire value chain; incremental strategies are not enough. These firms will thus have to come to terms with a process that is being discussed as re-engineering with regard to a fundamental restructuring of encrusted business structures in ICs (Hammer 1990). The concept of re-engineering goes back to experiences with greenfield sites, in which it is far easier to introduce new organizational principles than it is in older sites marked by ossified organizational-micropolicy structures.

The basic idea of re-engineering is the calling into question of all sequences and organizational patterns, i.e. a rejection of incremental change. The target system is outlined by the term lean management: flatter hierarchy, less division of labor, more responsibility for lower hierarchy levels, moves toward teamwork, and the like. This also includes approaches such as total cost management, which entails ascertaining detailed costs for all production phases and, e.g., product variants with an eye to identifying and eliminating cost factors that have hitherto gone unnoticed or been classified as fixed or overhead costs. Moreover, firms must learn to abstain from cost-plus pricing, and to start out by setting the required price and then dedicating their efforts to developing a product that can be manufactured at appropriate costs. These organizational measures for the most part offer a great potential for increased efficiency. Enterprises in batch industries in particular can in this way come closer to competitiveness; investments in new manufacturing techniques should be made following reorganization, which often makes it possible to lower them at the same time. The situation is different in process industries or, e.g., the textile industry, where both reorganization and high investment in new equipment are necessary in order to improve competitiveness.

In any case, the roads open to firms that have not yet reached competitive levels of are different from those open to firms that have already competed successfully in the world market (Table 1).

1. Marketing: When markets are opened, firms have to specialize far more intensively. Here it is helpful when they are as familiar as possible with their customers and their needs. This holds completely true for suppliers, who, ideally, cooperate closely with their customers as early as in the product development stage. And it is no less true for the manufacturers of final products. Enterprises in Western ICs have increasing realized in recent years that cooperation with customers in product development decisively improves the later sales chances of their products.

In particular in the East Asian NICs, it has been shown that firms can be highly successful when they stick to a defined succession of steps, with the aim of first concentrating on optimizing production, then learning product development, and only at a relatively late stage entering the arena of active marketing:

–   The first step is subcontracting, often for a customer from abroad, which involves manufacturing certain product components (or – in the case of less complex items – complete products) to the customer's exact specifications. The customer frequently provides

technical support aimed at selectively eliminating given bottlenecks in the subcontractor's operations.

– The second step is original equipment manufacturing (OEM), in
which the contractor manufactures his customer's complete product. The customer is responsible for product design and marketing.

– The third step is original design manufacturing (ODM). During the
1980s the number of firms in the East Asian NICs grew sharply
that not only manufacture to the specifications of foreign customers, but themselves develop products, and do so on the product
frontier (e.g. in the field of notebook computers). The foreign
partner's responsibility is no longer technology but only marketing.

2. Exports: Enterprises that have developed in a sheltered domestic
market and then initiate efforts aimed at exporting seldom meet with
success at once, for they at first tend to underestimate

– the competitive situation in their customer countries; i.e. they
proceed on the assumption that potential customers have been
waiting just for them. Only following initial unsuccessful attempts
to establish business relations do they learn to present their firms
in an adequate light;

– the degree of specialization expected by customers, appearing on
the scene with a product spectrum much to broad; only then do
they develop a specialization profile of their own;

– requirements as to quality, on-time delivery, and reliability;

– the advantages of continuous customer relations abroad, exporting
sporadically only when this (due to demand shortfalls in their
domestic market or shifts in exchange rates) appears particularly
attractive; only when, for specific reasons, a stable supply relationship has developed and the exporter has, for instance, received
technical assistance from his customer will the advantage entailed
by this relationship become manifest.

Table 1: How to improve efficiency and quality	
	Striving company
	Getting started
Employee involvement	Train heavily. Promote teamwork, but forget self-managed teams, which take heavy preparation. Limit employee empowerment to resolving customer complaints
Benchmarking	Emulate competitors, not world-class companies
New products	Rely mainly on customer input for ideas
Supply management	Choose suppliers mainly for price and reliability
New technology	Focus on its cost-reduction potential. Don't develop it - buy it
Manager and employee evaluation	Reward frontline workers for teamwork and quality
Quality progress	Concentrate on fundamentals. Identify processes that add value, simplify them, and move faster in response to customer and market demands. Don't bother using formal gauges of progress - gains will be apparent
Based on Ernst & Young / American Quality Foundation survey in North America, Germany, and Japan; quoted from Business Week, Dec. 7, 1992.	

Venturing company	Competitive company
Honing new skills	*Staying on top*
Encourage employees at every level to find ways to do their jobs better - and to simplify core operations. Set up a separate quality-assurance staff	Use self-managed, multiskilled teams that focus on horizontal processes such as logistics and product development. Limit training, mainly to new hires
Imitate market leaders and selected world-class companies	**Gauge product development, distribution, customer service vs. the world's best**
Use customer input, formal market research, and internal ideas	Base on customer input, benchmarking, and internal R&D
Select suppliers by quality certification, then price	Choose suppliers mainly for their technology and quality
Find ways to use facilities more flexibly to turn out a wider variety of products or services	Use strategic partnerships to diversify manufacturing
Base compensation for both workers and middle managers on contributions to teamwork and quality	Include senior managers in compensation schemes pegged to teamwork and quality
Meticulously document gains and further refine practices to improve value added per employee, time to market, and customer satisfaction	Keep documenting gains and further refine practices to improve value added per employee, time to market, and customer satisfaction

Bold fields: Activities that should reap the highest paybacks.

3. **Managing the transition toward the "networked" firm:** In inward-looking economies, closely networked relationships between specialized firms were the exception in the past. The rule was constituted by vertical integration within arm's-length relationships between firms. Enterprises increased their manufacturing depth because the local supply structure was underdeveloped; and the relations between suppliers and their customers were marked by mutual mistrust.

What is involved in building networks is not simply creating an interlinkage between firms which have until then operated beside one another, without any contact. Instead, it poses two challenges:

–   to strengthen potential suppliers who, owing to technological and organizational weaknesses, have not been regarded as competent suppliers;

–   to build continuous, trust-based relationships between firms whose history has been one of mistrust and conflict.

Final manufacturers are increasingly striving to reduce their vertical integration and to build supply networks, because they have no alternative – only through deverticalization can they improve their competitiveness. The development of suppliers is thus for them not an altruistic activity but grows out of the manifest necessities facing them. The condition for this is first the establishment of longer-term contractual relationships which provide both parties with a minimum of investment security. This basis enables the supplier to initiate a learning process which is supported in technical terms by his customer. The contractual relationship here is such that the success achieved by the supplier in learning and increasing his productivity also benefits his customer. It can be useful for the customer to provide annual cost targets geared to ensuring that the supplier's learning processes are adequate.

This model refers not alone to relationships between the manufacturer of the final product and his suppliers but to the whole of the supply pyramid. Suppliers too are faced with the challenge of reorganizing their own supply relationships and upgrading themselves into systems suppliers (i.e. suppliers of complete component assemblies). The goal must be to develop a multistage supply pyramid in which specific strengths can be built up at each stage.

4 Securing Close Interaction Between Government and Strategic Groups – the Institutional Dimension

4.1 Initiating Stakeholder Dialogues

Concepts of organization and governance relating to competition between firms which operate decentrally while government perceives its role exclusively as a regulatory and supervisory agency will not suffice to come to effective terms with industrial change in a phase of technological and worldwide economic upheaval. This applies in particular for industrially underdeveloped countries with relatively open economies in which the primarily weak national firms are forced to assert themselves vis-à-vis foreign direct investment and import competition from strong countries while at the same time attempting to grow into the world market, i.e. into the technological-industrial competition between the industrialized countries. An initially weak government must improve the conditions for the private sector, while at the same time coming to terms with fierce conflicts over redistribution.

The first step often involves overcoming, after a long period of one-sided domestic orientation, markedly rentist-corporatist patterns of organization. What is crucial here is a clear and unambiguous institutional separation of government, private economy, and society that enables actors capable of self-organization to grow.

When government separates itself from the tangle of interests constituted by particularist economic groups and strengthens the forces of the market, it will be in a position to reduce bureaucratic inflexibility and corruption and boost creative potentials. A relatively autonomous government whose economic technocracy is so insulated that it is in a position to pursue overall objectives will be able to impart impulses to industry and intermediary organizations that aim at developing a new orientation. The initial phase will be characterized at best by a small, consistent group of technocrats; over the medium term the task will be to build a reputable civil service.

Industrial associations and trade unions alike will have to free themselves from the fetters of their rentist-corporatist form of organization. To the extent that production- and export-oriented services hitherto provided by government are privatized, the firms will now demand the same for their associations, i.e. the dismantling of corporatist structures. Trade unions often defend corporatist labor relations ("government control against welfare payments and protection"), secure formal employment, and high wages and social security against non-organized and increasingly marginalized job-seekers; yet this is not sustainable. It is not infrequently government that provides the impulses toward overcoming the corporatist organization of capital and labor which has impeded the development of productivity and led to low rates of return on educational investments by inefficiently utilizing labor capacities. Government can encourage the development of independent self-help organization.

Institutional separation and a new mode of regulation can pave the way for cooperation between relatively autonomous partners representing their own interests in clearly defined paths. If this process fails to meet with adequate success, approaches involving learning by interacting are apt to prove unsuccessful, triggering abuses. It is especially the major firms that will utilize such approaches to lobby for special factors. Dialogue and interlinkage presuppose institutional autonomy – on the part of business and trade unions – and mobilization of specific development reserves on the part of the social actors. Within the framework of an independent though coordinated process of decision-making, government will refrain from intervening in areas typical of the market; the associations will respect government's relative autonomy. Clear rules create the trust required for any successful public-private sector consultation and cooperation.

The impetus toward developing more intensive government-business relations for the most part stems from government. It negotiates with domestic firms on investment projects and with foreign firms on their siting requirements. It develops discussion circles to prepare the conversion of production plants or research facilities of the armaments industry. Such groups also serve to improve framework conditions in favor of exporting industries and to prepare programs aimed at modernizing SMEs across all sectors. Once decentralization efforts show signs of success, discussion groups will emerge at the local and regional level, especially in heavily export-oriented regions. Not infrequently, wooing big business will constitute the focal point of consultations between government and industry. This purpose is served by the deliberation councils in East Asia which are organized along functional lines (e.g. financing) or according to industry (e.g. automobiles). They also strengthen the "competitive discipline" (Page 1992, 79 f) of industry and government.

Consultation between government and the other key actors is also geared to building up rapid communications with an eye to using information transmission to heighten the transparency of the manner in which all of the partners proceed. The discussions will initially be strongly oriented toward practical considerations and provide industry with concrete benefits (regulation, taxation, access to credit, coordination of export strategies and investment). Government consults with industry on the export-oriented development of material infrastructure and involves it in the reform and development of educational, R&D, and financing institutions (coresponsibility and partial financing). Government, industry, and trade unions cooperate in building a flexible labor market which safeguards export objectives ("high quality and low costs"). Efforts aimed at optimizing labor and manpower qualification will be stepped up with an eye to supporting corporate efficiency.

The most important initial achievements aimed toward national industrialization consist in creating a basic consensus on shaping the environment in which firms operate as well as an overall development strategy, in particular organizational patterns. This first jump in potential is possible as long as what is focused on is not the variously strong ideological economic and regulatory concepts of ICs that may contribute to macroeconomic stabilization, but the innovative organizational patterns of ICs, in particular as regards the best practice organization of production. This inclines the dialogue toward cooperative, flexible, innovation-oriented and focused concepts of organization and governance. The dialogue serves to achieve agreement on the direction in which the industrialization process is to move and the sequences involved in the process as well to reach, again and again, agreement on particulars with an eye to shaping the various elements of the industrial system.

4.2   Establishing Cooperative Relationships Between Government and Strategic Groups

What is required to transform discussion groups dealing above all with concrete problems into established consultative councils is an effective government development agency (type: MITI/Japan, Economic Planning Board/Republic of Korea) which prepares the ground for an overall concept of economic and social policy as well as for the various elements and stages needed to implement it. The councils serve above all to tie the groups of public and private actors into the overall concepts, to concentrate medium- and long-term economic and technological objectives, and to create the groundwork for implementing an increasingly differentiated pattern of strategies.

This dialogue is doubtless facilitated when it is accompanied by a redistribution of economic resources in favor of the strategically relevant private-sector actors participating in it. In the Republic of Korea, for instance, government has made scarce resources, above all bank credit and foreign exchange, available chiefly to national conglomerates and initiated the establishment of so-called general trading firms. Once a process of dynamic industrialization was underway, however, the government curtailed the concentration processes in industry, e.g. by stepping up its encouragement of SMEs.

Government's role in the dialogue is to generate impulses, to coordinate, and to provide direction. Government reduces internal and external obstacles that prevent industry from bringing national locational and competitive advantages to bear. What is called for is not for government authorities, with their limited knowledge, to draft indicative plans. What is required is an active, anticipatory and dialogue-based structural policy which emerges out of intensive interaction between the partners in dialogue and is tailored to developing and bringing to bear the national competitive advantage. Important elements of any shaping of structures with the long-term goal of national systemic integration include:

–   reduction of the gap, for the most part wide, between public governance and corporate decision-making, with the goal of creating the conditions for a strategic corporate management dedicated to developing world-market competence;

–   intensification of the relationships between financial sector and industrial sector; the probability to achieve this can be improved by including banks in the dialogue or providing state guarantees;

–   inclusion of industry and, if possible, the trade unions in the process of institutional reform and development (e.g. of public vocational schools) and building a competition-oriented service sector;

–   a dynamic process of cluster-building; improving the network capabilities of self-help organizations within the business and the labor sector; intensification of network-building via local, regional, and national administration; cost reduction in major and mid-size firms via supplier networks and joint organization so as to mobilize export potentials;

–   implementation of a strategy of spatially polarized growth, in part via a policy of industrial location and encouragement which contributes to shaping spatial structures. This strategy creates, above all in first-order industrial agglomeration centers, favorable conditions for the development of spatially concentrated, functionally interlinked systems of production and innovation. It also strengthens second- and third-order agglomeration centers. Selective expansion of vocational-training, R&D, financial, and export-promotion institutions is used to support the formation of spatial focuses in favor of specific priority sectors. The allocation-related goals of the strategy include "cost reduction", "joint learning process", and not infrequently "joint representation of interests" vis-à-vis the outside world.

In view of scarcity of resources and lack of competence, the public-sector/private-sector dialogue is directed toward clarifying the question: "How much selectivity?", i.e. in strengthening global and regional players, encouraging promising fields of industrial specialization, in providing impulses for regions already strong in exporting, and in supporting communities of small firms, e.g. in utilizing flexible manufacturing systems. Selectivity results from the ability of government to assess public and private capabilities, to provide orientation in terms of the organizational-technical patterns of successful ICs, and to accept the shaping of structures by the partners in the institutionalized dialogue. This process requires positions to be redetermined again and again in the light of domestic and foreign requirements and joint action to be the rule in a wide range of fields. One special problem consists in the fact that the dialogue that was first conducted in East Asia between a limited number of "strategic partners" today appears to require an early inclusion of the local level, of mid-size firms and important clusters.

4.3   Encouraging the Establishment of Development-Minded Intermediary Institutions of Capital and Labor

Radical change grows out of market and world-market orientation: Economic associations, chambers of industry and commerce, and trade unions become self-help-organizations that offer services to their members. This applies, in close cooperation with business firms, for the diffusion of new production and marketing concepts or the representation of industry interests at trade fairs and exhibitions at home and abroad. The cooperation between government and industry associations should as far as possible by guided by branch-wide restructuring processes. Industry associations cooperate to support the competitiveness of world-market-oriented production chains (e.g. cattle breeding-leather-shoes). A high capacity for self-organization on the part of groups of private actors at the local, regional, and national level is a prerequisite for any effective representation of concrete group interests as well as for dialogue and interlinkage, both intergroup and with government.

Within the framework of corporate modernization, a new type of industrial worker emerges who meets the demands placed on him, despite low wage levels. Young, efficient core teams with higher educational levels support the new production concepts winning ground in particular in export-oriented industrial firms. It is above all these firms that give rise to growing demand for skilled workers. The process begins with intensive qualification on the job or abroad, thus making it possible to successfully utilize the latest lean manufacturing systems. In a second phase, the number of domestic and foreign firms upgrading operations to world quality levels increases. Over the medium term, the demand for skilled labor leads to an expansion of extra-plant vocational training and advanced training.

Government creates a labor market that is efficient, flexible, and responsive to changing conditions. New regulations provide for unimpeded access to and exit from the labor market as well as a high level of labor-force mobility while at the same time not stimulating an overly degree of turnover. At the same time, industrial safety is improved and accident, unemployment and health insurance systems are expanded. Government is responsible for limiting the growth of public-sector employment, i.e. it is responsible for preventing the mis-allocation of manpower in the public sector typical under conditions of inward orientation. Government will advance labor-force qualification by investing in training, at the same time supporting the trade-union discussion on optimizing labor in the interest of corporate efficiency, on job creation, with an eye to exploiting the crucial comparative advantage – the reservoir of manpower willing to learn and to perform – as well as on a reorganization and reorientation of the trade unions. In addition, government will secure a higher return on public investment in education by concentrating funding on elementary and vocational schools.

Following the initial phase, in which a consistent low-wage policy is inevitable, government contributions to realizing uniform wage-setting practices assumes great significance. An orientation in terms of East and Southeast Asian countries makes sense here; the elements include: a base wage relatively independent of corporate profits and performance-based bonuses keyed to concrete firm performance; furthermore, wages responsive to changes in the demand for labor, which permit rapid adjustment to external macroeconomic shocks. The normally strong tendencies toward highly selective labor markets can only gradually be reduced and redirected toward a uniform price of labor. Any reduction of the gap between the wages for agricultural labor and unskilled labor or between skilled and unskilled labor – as in Taiwan – will, however, remain a long-term objective in most countries, provided that the various groups of actors are able to create jointly the conditions essential to achieving it.

The labor market can be further integrated once a relatively high rate of economic growth has led to rising real wage levels. Wage increases for unskilled labor gradually erode international competitiveness in labor-intensive manufactured goods. The demand for labor will tend increasingly to be skill-intensive, because exporting firms will shift into more technologically sophisticated, skill-intensive goods. Assuming that population growth slows, this development will be supported by slower growth of the labor force.

Even if government policy is to let markets work, it is faced with tasks in addition to those just named. Government is coresponsible not only for a creative discussion on shaping labor relations but also for acceptance of the new strategy by both industrial and labor organizations. A high level of acceptance first leads to a rapid reduction of cost-pushing behavioral patterns such as absenteeism, high fluctuation rates, and uneven workmanship, and thus to a high level of efficiency achieved via performance and reduced labor unrest. Government represents the common interest in improving international competitiveness and modernizing and democratizing labor relations while providing for basic social security for the population as a whole. Government at the same time works toward the goal of dynamic social integration.

The efforts of the trade unions to find a new orientation will tend to differ considerably. Some, with an eye to US business union concepts or Japanese company union concepts, will concentrate on firms as the central field for negotiating working conditions. Others will look to the experience of European labor relations, even though there is no tradition of autonomous collective bargaining and negotiating working conditions in talks between representatives of employer and employee organizations. It is not uncommon for different patterns of trade union organization to exist side by side.

"Distortions of competition" in the world market due to differences in labor costs and social standards are unavoidable. Any such distortion based on restrictions of basic rights (freedom of association, collective bargaining), viz. the repression of labor organizations, is not acceptable in the international community. In all countries, solving conflicts cooperatively at the local, regional, and national level, including labor unions, contributes to achieving the new technical-organizational paradigm. Any successful increase in efficiency via improvements in cost, quality, and time saving processes which are able to mobilize high levels of competitive reserves also depends on the interest of trade unions in increasing productivity, and thus increasing wages.

5   The Regional Dimension of International Competitiveness

5.1   The Rationale of (Sub)Regional Cooperation and Integration

The world economy is moving toward a small number of trading groups (EEC, NAFTA, perh. Yen Zone). The supply and demand conditions for competition-oriented economies can be improved distinctly in a regional framework. In particular, the medium-sized ICs of western Europe have been at work building a major economic zone with an eye to increasing the investment, growth, and competitive chances of businesses. The completion of the EC single market entailed a jump in concentration aimed at decreasing the scale-related disadvantages of European firms in comparison with those of the USA and Japan. The creation of the European Economic Space is intended to provide firms with relatively stable demand conditions for a major share of their products. Sharply increasing the funds available to finance EC research and technology policy is intended to close the gap in the utilization of new technologies. The volume of support provided by the individual member states is not sufficient to achieve and defend a technological lead in many important high-tech fields against the US and Japanese economies, which are far better funded (Schmalholz and Penzkofer 1993, 25).

As IC trade and integration groups are extended toward the south, the growth chances of the countries involved (e.g. Spain in the EC or Mexico in NAFTA) improve. The East and Southeast Asian "early imitators" with strong technological-industrial dynamics are seeking orientation in Japan's pattern of development, and entertain close economic ties to Japan, while at the same time benefiting in particular from the industrial division of labor with the US. The powerful industrial subpoles in these countries are reinforcing the tendency to form a regional group around Japan. Thus, for instance, the jump in investment in the Republic of Korea and Taiwan in Southeast Asia in recent years has stimulated intra-regional trade. At the same time, the nations of Southeast Asia are building a subregional free trade zone of their own. The process of group formation will continue; there are voices that advocate including countries from Central-Eastern Europe and the Mediterranean area in the EC and creating a pan-American FTZ.

The efforts of one-sidedly inward-looking countries to achieve an "integration against the world market" were unsuccessful because industry was subjected to little pressure to integrate. To avoid having to confront the regional groups of the North in isolation, DC are today making efforts directed toward mutual (sub)regional cooperation (e.g. MERCOSUR, ASEAN). They are seeking to improve jointly the demand and supply conditions of their industry, in particular the conditions required for cost-lowering industrial mass production. The goals of the open regionalism of the DCs is similar to those in the North, although they are encountering greater obstacles and more resistance.

Regional markets often present an essential learning and testing ground for exporting industrial goods to exacting IL markets. Even more than their firms, the DCs themselves need a large market dimension as a testing ground to prepare for their attempts to advance into the world market with technology-intensive products. More and more Latin American countries are succeeding in becoming regional players, for instance. In MERCOSUR, the beginnings of a subregional industrial subcontracting are also becoming visible. Furthermore, trading firms in some countries have also started exporting products from neighboring countries ("indirect export"). In addition, service firms (tourism services, business consulting) are growing into a subregional dimension.

Domestic demand is a very significant factor for foreign industrial corporations. If it grows at the subregional level, subsidiaries are able to modernize in organizational and technical terms, in order then to produce more intensively for export into third countries. It is in particular subsidiaries of automotive corporations that have been able surmount bottlenecks in demand, which can occur even in countries as large as Brazil, by forming corporate interlinkages, via subregional specialization, and by seeking integration into worldwide corporate strategies. When regional demand is adequate, they expand their local advantages derived from interlinkage, e.g. via networks with suppliers and maintenance firms.

Regional cooperation and integration strengthen first-, second-, and third-order agglomeration centers, which in turn interlink and radiate out into their own frontier areas and peripheries. Intraregional specialization encourages the formation of spatial-economic structures and shapes spatial industrial structures. The first-order industrial agglomeration centers grow to form technological and industrial cores with regional and international relevance. They entail the great advantages of "agglomeration" and "proximity" on which innovation industries rely. The firms in them are in possession of high levels of experience in utilizing economies of scale and flexibility. These centers experience very close interlinkages between firms, R&D institutions and financial institutions, and between producers and consumers. The differentiated demand in industrial cores is an important condition for international competitiveness.

The development of favorable supply conditions for industry proceed from the first-order centers. The second- and third-order centers are not so likely to succeed in creating, on their own initiative (or even with foreign support), supply conditions adequate to launch a broad-based advance into the high-tech sphere. These centers are responsible for the specialization process in their national economies and regions, increases in productivity in industries based there having for the most part provided the initial impulses. The specialization chances of such firms are improved when they are closely linked to first-order regional industrial centers.

But regional integration does not only strengthen industrial agglomeration centers. It also permits integration of national economies which lack sufficient potential to form such centers, or which in some cases even lack an industrialization perspective of their own. In the former case, the growing functionality and quality of agglomeration centers improve the chances of major and mid-size regional firms in industries engaged in mass production to grow out into competitive positions in the world market. In the latter case, the chances increase of taking advantage of the regional industrial location policy of foreign and domestic firms and of utilizing regional complementarities to build – as world-market orientation grows – regional complementary industries which may grow to form "developed peripheries" (Esser 1980).

5.2   Formulating Regional Cooperation and Integration Schemes

The currently emerging forms of (sub)regional cooperation and integration in DC regions seem to indicate that we are in a phase preparatory to the development of free-trade groups. The first phase will above all see a reduction in individual regions of specific disadvantages. The conditions for regional interaction are improved by the emergence of political parties, industrial associations, and trade unions with a regional dimension. This strengthens any common political vision; "democracy", for instance, is the sine qua non for membership in an integration project. Moreover, the threat of a replacement of multilateralism with a system of managed trade and closed regional blocks can be averted in this way. Regional endeavors also aim to encounter the threats posed by a deterioration of prices for raw materials (oil, coffee) and protectionism in industrial regions (bananas, textiles, steel, etc.)

1. In some DC regions, regional cooperation clearly contributes to improving the supply conditions for industry. Market and world-market orientation generate considerable pressure toward reorganization and development of physical infrastructure. This in turn intensifies efforts directed toward expanding border-crossing infrastructure:

- Joint utilization of modern ports often makes expensive investment unnecessary or lowers transportation costs (e.g. export from Mendoza/Argentina via Chilean ports).

- Joint energy projects (bilateral retaining dams, oil or gas networks) contribute to lowering costs, sometimes to the utilization of more ecologically compatible energies as well. In some exceptional cases, joint energy policies are emerging that are aimed at forming (sub)regional energy-supply systems.

– One essential condition for integration, both international and regional, is modernization of the telecommunications sector. This is the necessary condition for any coordination between corporate headquarters in various regions of the world as well as for any networking of suppliers, manufacturers, and retailers, on the regional level as well. It is also a condition for the regional and international marketing activities of trading firms and the smooth operation of capital markets with a pronounced regional and international dimension.

– Higher education and vocational training as well as R&D cooperation ("technological integration") should be coordinated on the regional level, and they should be oriented at economically relevant areas (e.g. technical and managerial ongoing training, postgraduate studies in science and engineering). The number of projects aiming at focalizing regionally available know-how inside regional centers of excellence appears to be rising.

2. Bilateral, subregional, and regional – and in exceptional cases international – FTZs create larger markets. They in this way intensify the investment interest of domestic and foreign firms. FTZs facilitate the adjustment and expansion processes facing exports, difficult in the initial phases. FTZs between ICs and DCs (NAFTA) enlarge the dimensions of the market available, above all to the latter. In view of an ensured access to the IC market, specialization will intensify, which will in the long run amount to "associated industrialization". This applies to job processing by subsidiaries no less than for industries like the automotive industry in Mexico, which can achieve comparative productivity and quality at 1/10 of US labor costs.

The attractiveness of FTZs lies – apart from initial boosts to exports – in additional arrangements in various areas of cooperation (non-trade gains). Some examples are the improvement of industrial safety and environmental protection in low-wage countries, enforcement of investment codes and legal regulations on intellectual property, and agreements on competition, subsidy, and public procurement policies. FTZs intensify existing dynamics by safeguarding institutionally flows of capital, goods, and services. If they are developed between ICs and DCs, they facilitate the take-over of relatively labor- or capital-intensive industries from ICs, while contributing little – at least in the initial phases – to dismantling the worldwide system of graduated comparative advantages.

If FTZs generate sophisticated rules on origin and local content, this can lead to the development of effective new instruments of protection. In addition, they also entail restrictions on second best options when they are regarded as a substitute for national competitive strategies with an international dimension. To the extent that a liberal trade climate exists, the trade-creating effects of FTZs should not be over-estimated. In some cases, FTZs contribute to improving the conditions for the emergence of strong subregional free-trade groups. They often also create favorable conditions for subsequent currency unions/CUs.

3. The joint external tariffs in CUs do away with the need for rules on origin. If the "dominant economy" is stable and dynamic, a suitable framework will emerge for joint industrial development. To be sure, there are difficulties involved in the economic and social imbalances between the member states (and regions):

–   The weaker countries seek to reduce their adjustment burdens (exemption clauses, compensation mechanisms). At the outset, however, the main concern of DCs cannot be to reduce interre-gional imbalances; the task is to give rise to a generally higher level of growth dynamics. In a medium- and long-term pers-pective, an interregional compensation mechanism can be used to address the social imbalances between member states and their regions (e.g. via regional funds).

–   The subpoles will be unable to count on any subspecialization, since any such attempts would – in part due to the inadequate pull exercised by the first-order centers – not essentially improve their siting and growth conditions. Their dynamics are for a certain time primarily dependent on the intensity of their world-market specialization.

(Sub)regional markets represent a base for industrial production of big firms, if there is a demand potential that makes it possible to realize minimum-efficient scales (Oman 1992, 12), the relevance of which is in most industries not diminished by lean manufacturing. CUs between small countries will not create any "optimal economic zones" or strong free-trade groups. They will for the most part not even reach the scale of moderately large countries. Since this will fail to give rise to any autonomous internationally meaningful functional zone, the option that remains is to join, simultaneously if possible, a neighboring regional group (e.g. CACM and CARICOM via FTZ with Mexico and, if feasible, with NAFTA as a whole).

5.3   The Role of the Public and Private Sector in Regional Cooperation and Integration Schemes

1. Regional dialogue between governments is of great significance. A joint political framework with consultation and coordination mechanisms makes it possible to pursue a pragmatic approach to regional and world-market-oriented coordination and cooperation. An institutional core assumes the required task of "soft control".

The short-term goal is to develop a joint vision on the principles and methods of regional political and economic cooperation. It is furthermore necessary to imbed regional institutions, including subregional FTZs and CUs, in a joint perspective. The focus of the dialogue consists of three topics:

–   the economic-policy discussion, which is aimed at improving, in a fruitful exchange of information, the conditions for the coordination of economic policies and laying the groundwork for drafting a joint regional regulatory concept;

–   understanding on the rough pattern of intraregional division of labor, which can lead, among other things, to cooperative projects aimed at fostering market-related R&D activities and jointly building precompetitive structures which at the same time improve the conditions for world-market specialization;

– joint efforts at improving international negotiation potentials, on which a good number of market positions are dependent; within the framework of a constructive regionalism based on a growing consensus between government and industry, it is possible to improve the conditions necessary for an enlightened regional economic nationalism, which can be channeled via strategic negotiations with other regional trade and integration groups.

2. Market and world-market orientation see a growth in the interest of industry in expanding the scope of its investment and growth activities via FTZs and, above all, CUs. The deregulation and privatization of state-owned firms lead to a process of concentration in the private sector, thus strengthening, among others, domestic industrial corporations. In view of narrow domestic demand, both foreign investors and major national firms will push to expand markets.

As a result of surpluses in the world market, domestic and foreign corporations, in particular in petrochemical complexes, integrated steelworks, and the automotive industry, will press forward in this direction. Banks, insurance firms, trading firms, or consulting firms will also demand equal opportunities on the intraregional level. For innovation industries, above all high-tech firms, a larger domestic market is essential to be able to survive in international competition. To achieve positions in the intraregional race for sites and growth, it is often important for the investment and development opportunities offered by CUs first give rise to a more pronounced orientation of the financial sector in terms of the needs of the productive sector.

3. The ICs should, in their own interest, step up their efforts to encourage regional integration in the South:

– The development of regional groups in the North and growing protectionism among the industrial countries clearly indicate that the effectiveness of a model of international integration based on undifferentiated division of labor will, in many industries, soon prove inadequate. An open, constructive regionalism – in both North and South – contributes to reducing the turbulences in the multilateral system of trade.

– Integration increases the power of the South's industrial agglomeration centers to form cores and creates demand levels attractive for domestic and foreign firms, which can reduce the pressure on extraregional industrial exports.

– In integrated regions, the size- and efficiency-related disadvantages of many small and mid-size states, frequently a result of the process from which they emerged as states, will decrease in significance.

– One other factor is that the development of FTZs and CUs reduces arms races, and can sometimes even lead to military cooperation and the development of (sub) regional security alliances – this should induce the ICs to promote resolutely regional integration in DC regions. The fact alone that in some DC regions border conflicts, at times intensive, will fade into insignificance, rendering superfluous any regional arms races, justifies integration projects.

6   From Comparative Advantage to Systemic Competitiveness – a Quest for Visions, Strategies, and Continuous Interactive Learning

1. An economy's international competitiveness is contingent on a country's overall technical-organizational-social profile. In many developing countries this overall profile is characterized by fragmentation, at times even by social disintegration. Under such conditions industrialization efforts will hardly succeed. Industrial underdevelopment can only be overcome when societies, based on consensus, succeed in undertaking deliberate efforts to focus their forces and develop them with reference to guiding principles and visions.

The guiding principle of "systemic competitiveness" has chances of being realized above all when "market" (instrumental rationality) and "organization" (social orientation) have one direction of thrust and are closely coupled in such a way as to encourage the mobilization of synergy and correction and adjustment potentials. The state's task is to coordinate, in a well-defined search and learning process, the relationship between the competitive orientation and strengthening of industrial locations, societal development (with a view to the social and political dimension), and ecological sustainability, in this way creating the conditions required for a concept of a managed economic, social, and ambiental change.

2. It is hardly possible to state *a priori* where the specialization opportunities open to developing countries might lie; in particular, the analysis of the factor endowments of specific country groups or individual countries will not provide this information. Certainly, countries in an initial phase of the development of systemic competitiveness will above all have to exploit their given factor endowments. But under the conditions of radical technical and organizational change a more broadly based analysis is needed to identify the sectors of industry and technology that should receive development priority. Any such analysis must include existing industrial and technological potentials, current market trends, and the strategies of competing countries. It is on this basis possible to define industrialization priorities, i.e. the industrial cores in which world-market competence is to be achieved, and it is essential here to promote the development of functionally interlinked and, as the case may be, regionally concentrated production and innovation networks and to prevent the emergence of industrial and technological enclaves. In other words, instead of pursuing a strategy of marching through the sectors, which results from a strict application of the principle of comparative cost advantages, an industrial strategy should set its sights at marching within the sectors, i.e. be geared to developing world-market-specialized industrial cores and successively increasing their size rather than their number.

3. The task of strengthening the competitiveness of an economy requires in particular dedicated, continuous learning on the part of

government, firms, and intermediary organizations. The objective is to develop a competitive cooperative system, i.e. a market economy constantly revised and heightened through dialogue and continuous development of the social and ecological dimensions of economy and society.

What is essential to achieving this goal is to establish economic management as a process of interactive learning. The market acts as a motor driving rationalization, government as a motor linking economic and overall social factors. Government, in strategic pragmatism, represents the model, enforces the pattern of organization, and brings the groups of actors together. The organizational pattern of "interactive learning" is strengthened by imbedding the formation of structures in a process consisting of dialogue and complex interlinkage. Interaction aims at an industrial structure and a social system that make it possible to concentrate national forces in favor of systemic competitiveness, reducing poverty, and sustaining development.

4. Government must be relatively autonomous, strong, and efficient if it is to provide impulses toward gaining acceptance of the model, of new standards for industry and society as a whole, of patterns of behavior oriented toward consensus and cooperation, of institutions enabling a dynamic interactive learning, and of intermediary organizations that advance it. It is often essential to join together structural elements which are already existent though isolated and oriented in terms of particularist interests to form an economic and overall social context. One further task is to re-create socioeconomic structures – down to and including civil societies with their complex rule systems.

The first challenge facing many countries is to incorporate into an economic societal context structural organizational elements, or islands of efficiency, that already exist, though they are dispersed and oriented to particular interests:

– The firms' interest in short-term maximization of profits actors must be subordinated to the goal of medium- and long-term improvement of international competitiveness and capturing growing market shares abroad, this being based on the development of production and innovation networks and the overall interlinkage of groups of national groups of actors.

– Labor is not only a cost factor. It is at the same time human capital that deserves and requires investment. Capital and labor should try to overcome an antagonistic relationship, even if they do pursue – on the basis of a shared underlying consensus – their own interests.

Finally, this foundation serves the purpose of further developing socioeconomic structures – down to and including civil society with the complex rules governing it.

5. Public welfare is not simply a goal of lesser importance in the overall strategy and its implementation. The overall strategy makes possible, from the very outset, concrete steps toward a community-based system. Social interlinkage is advanced together with economic interlinkage. In weakly organized DCs it is essential that various groups of actors first develop in their specific fields favorable patterns of behavior and organization keyed to rapid and increasingly complex learning. Then, government, industry, meso-institutions, and intermediary institutions can together create the conditions for cumulative learning processes and continuous interactive learning. Government has the tasks of integrating social groups, within the framework of an orientation of society in terms of a technical civilization, into processes of learning and decision-making. Systemic competitiveness calls for a high level of organization of a society, enabling rapid progress toward a creative and in many ways community-related civil society.

6. Conclusion: The formation of structures in economy and society is oriented in terms of the development of groups of strong actors:

– an autonomous and efficient government,

– a highly competitive industry,

– intermediary institutions that make possible a democratic interplay of forces.

All three groups of actors are, however, not "system actors" in the initial phases of industrial and social development: the national private sector must come to terms with foreign corporations at home and with import competition to find its way to the world market. Government is faced with the challenge of having to create for industry a favorable macroeconomic and specific climate and at the same time mobilize and organize society. Because democratic and liberal patterns of behavior are often not rooted in everyday life, is essential to build a participatory "strong democracy" (Barber 1984) which can likewise contribute to securing the direction of economic and overall social development. What is essential is not for a highly interventionist and corporative-minded government to bind forces together in authoritarian fashion, but a determined leadership group, an effective state constitution, a professional bureaucracy, and a strategic vision aimed at joining isolated economic, social and political forces with the objective of achieving world-economic and world-political advantages stemming from learning and organization.

It is the strategic orientation of system actors in network-like relationship patterns that first makes it possible to increasingly replace traditional hierarchic patterns with forms of horizontal cooperation. To the extent that intermediary organizations ensure a democratic interplay of forces, it is possible for a constructive power to emerge that, while running counter to state and industry, at the same time shares its direction of motion. Balancing competitiveness and modes of cooperative action is facilitated by inclusion of intermediary organizations in dialogue and interlinkage. A democratic *ensemble* heightens the synergetic effects that make it possible to achieve technical-industrial gains, possibly even to gain and extend technological leads. It is important to balance more strongly and as quickly as possible the three goals of "systemic competitiveness", "social justice", and "sustainability of development".

Obstacles and resistance must be expected in building an economic and social system. Relapses into authoritarian patterns cannot be ruled out. As a result of the great economic demands involved, the risk of economistic foreshortening is great, especially if weak traditions of community-relatedness are involved. Even when groups of actors interact, faulty decisions cannot be ruled out. Strategic options and key issues change rapidly in the process of industrial and social development. A strategic vision that includes precise knowledge of the rough pattern of industrialized countries makes it easier to adjust and re-adjust policies. A high level of dynamics is made possible by success in tailoring an autonomous economic and social profile, since, despite external disruptive potentials, it is the endogenous factors that count in the end.

Part IV Competitiveness, Social Justice, and Sustainable Development

1   Social and Ecological Responsibility – the National and Global Dimension

The "social question" emerged in connection with the first push for innovation and industrialization in the industrialized countries. There it was in part defused through the organized pressure brought to bear by the persons affected, government responses to this pressure, and the further progress of industrial development; this entailed introducing and expanding the social dimension of the market economy, which contributed to preventing and reducing social imbalances. These days, the demands growing out of the worldwide success of the market system in most competitive and innovative industrialized countries lead – especially in the transitional phase – to an intensification of social problems. Responses to the demands posed by new waves of innovation may lead to a reintensification of social imbalances, even in the industrialized countries.

In the developing countries the "social question" is far more urgent, not the least since these countries are faced with the greatest share of population growth. In them, too, expectations and levels of demands that will certainly not diminish, exposing the groups of political and economic actors to growing pressure to improve national transformation capacities. At the same time, when the state and the business sector are highly efficient in organizational terms, relatively low levels of wages and social services constitute an advantage in international competition.

The environmental burdens that emerged in connection with the economic exploitation of the second to the last wave of invention and innovation were so severe that the world saw itself faced with the question as to the "responsibility for the continued existence of the whole" (Jonas 1993). Production processes and products were energy- and raw-material-intensive; industrial development led to a seemingly boundless expansion of individual consumption that was restrained only by the wealth and incomes available. Three factors made it possible to restrain the consumption of resources: the emerging wave of innovation, national, but also international, environmental policies, and the collapse of one-sidedly inward-looking organizational patterns, which were particularly detrimental to the environment in that they failed to exploit even elementary efficiency potentials. Still, the environmental problem continues to grow, and will continue to do so as long as the expansion of individualist consumption patterns in the industrialized countries continues unchecked and the dynamic industrialization in East and Southeast Asia, including China, continues to be associated with lower levels – low relative to the industrialized countries – of resource and environmental protection.

But there is, it appears, no alternative to the strategy of harnessing the new chances offered by industrial reorganization as a means of increasing resource efficiency and using consciousness-building ("new consumer ethics") and regulation to check the dynamism driving the expansion of individualism and relate it back to the quality of society's contribution toward finding solutions to economic and social problems with an eye to sustainable development. It will not be possible to halt the now global dynamics of science, technical change, and industry; all the greater, therefore, the significance attaching to the revision of the "Bacon Project" (Schäfer 1993) aimed at opening up the way to a new synthesis between economy and ecology. At the core of this revision is the question as to the basic features of production and consumption, and thus at the same time the issue of the relationship between state, producers, consumers, and intermediary organization.

The organizational pattern that makes systemic competitiveness possible does not aim chiefly to master social and ecological problems.

But without sufficient organizational capacity the outcome of the struggle against poverty and environmental degradation is apt to be rather meager. The emerging pattern seems to represent a framework suited to shaping the relationship between labor and capital, growth and redistribution, and economy and ecology, and doing so in a way consonant with changing economic and overall social needs.

2   Combing Efficiency and Social Equity

A competition-oriented economy and efficient government make it possible, within the framework of a long-term strategy, to implement a complex set of dovetailed policies aimed at reducing absolute poverty, expanding employment, and increasing the level of domestic demand. When dynamic industrial development is realized, it is possible, as can be seen in East and Southeast Asia, to achieve a system of basic social security and a clear-cut increase in employment via some such set of policies, despite major progress in productivity. Small and mid-size countries such as Chile have, even in the face of a low level of industrial dynamics, reduced absolute poverty and unemployment while sustaining high medium-term economic growth rates; however, the multiplier effects stemming from the dynamic economic sector are limited. Presupposing the political will to do so, many other DCs will be able to achieve a system of basic social security, and with it a reduction of absolute poverty.

1. Population policy: An annual growth rate of the population of 2.7 % and more and the labor force of 3 – 4 %, as expected in Honduras or Nicaragua in the period from 1991 – 2000, indicates that government is in a position neither to implement the required set of policies nor to contribute toward building a competition-oriented industrial sector and an efficient service sector. The share of persons living in absolute poverty and persons working in the informal sector will continue to rise in such countries. If, however, the unused potentials of self-determined family planning are fully utilized, the demographic growth rate can, in the medium-term, be reduced to 1.5 – 1 % p.a. Since this case would make possible an economic growth rate distinctly above the demographic growth rate as well as substantial progress in development, priority ought to be accorded to high levels of private and public investment in order to reduce population growth. Population policy is a national problem of the highest order.

2. Employment policy: A minimum long-term growth rate of over 5 – 6 % p.a. is required to reduce the employment problem and other problems directly or indirectly linked to it (high levels of domestic migration or urbanization): growth rates of this magnitude would neutralize population growth of some 2 % and make it possible to partake of productivity growth stemming from international economic factors. Only above this level would additional employment opportunities emerge. To be sure, competition-oriented industrialization would offer the chance of far higher rates of productivity growth.

3. Social policy:

–   Private-sector participation eases the burden of the public social services and gives rise to competition in the health-care, educational, and social-security sectors. In the case of private retirement schemes, current pension payments are financed via investment returns on a capital fund fed by the contributions made by members. Such pension funds have proven to be important instruments for invigorating the capital market, in tendency also for raising the savings rate and long-term lending. Their workability depends on the institution of a government supervisory authority to provide for adherence to legally binding, risk-limiting guidelines covering the use of the funds and prevent mismanagement through corruption.

–   Public social policy is concentrated on poverty-reduction targets (initially via social funds). Centrally regulated, the structure of social policy is shaped in municipalities and regions, the central government supporting the initiatives developed by local authorities of low-income regions.

— As a rule, there is plenty of room to raise the efficiency and quality of social services, e.g. lowering costs by introducing competition in public procurement.

— Social policy should also be more closely geared to the needs of industry. This is true in particular for selective vocational training conceived with reference to the clusters of the economy and avoiding any overburdening of the economy due to social policy.

4. Budgetary policy: Effective basic services can be achieved in the medium-term with a poverty-oriented public social policy via redistribution of around 1 – 1.5 % of GDP p.a. Budgetary policy should at the same time permit a high level of private investment (and thus future orientation as opposed to consumption, i.e. orientation toward the present) by, for example, disproportionately raising public expenditures for health care, education, and R&D as well as pursuing social goals via restructuring in the individual policy areas, e.g. in favor of elementary and vocational schooling at the expense of university financing.

5. Employment policy: Flexible yet increasingly integrated labor markets ease the task of restructuring low-wage sectors to form dynamic industries.

6. SME policy: Tax incentives and medium-term to long-term credits are required to modernize relatively labor-intensive SME clusters (e.g. the shoe industry), entire branches of industry, as well as production chains when this at the same time involves organization for export. One question yet to be clarified is the extent to which relatively labor- and capital-intensive processes can be combined.

7. Policy toward the informal sector: Microenterprises assume great significance during transitions crises. Claiming little public social support, they create jobs while government and formal firms are shedding them. When a high level of economic growth is achieved, the informal sector shrinks. Encouragement of microenterprises improves their chances of returning to the formal sector and – there is no lack of examples – even of growing into export to neighboring countries. The dynamics in the informal sector will, as long as the sector exists, be shaped largely by the dynamics in the competition-oriented economic sector. The organizational level of the poor population and the social and political pressure of the intermediary organizations influenced by it, is in all countries of great significance for reducing extreme poverty as well as for raising wages, although this does not hold true with regard to the development of employment in the productivity-oriented economic sector.

8. Sectoral policies: Structural reforms in the agricultural sector and high levels of investment toward the end of forming human capital clearly contribute, as can be seen in East Asia, to reducing extreme poverty and the employment problem. If the agricultural sector is efficiently organized for export (e.g. via trading firms), it will give rise to additional jobs (Chile). Transition from a long period of one-sided domestic industrial orientation can entail significant losses of jobs (manufacturing employment in Latin America 1980: 11, 1990: 10 million), which requires flanking social funds.

9. Research policy: In view of the – for the foreseeable future – major tendency toward a growing employment problem in industrial and developing countries when "new technologies" are employed, extensive reflections on the relations of the factors labor and capital, which would go beyond the scope of this report, will prove to be of great significance.

3   Combining Efficiency and Sustainability

150 years of industrialization have led to an enormous ecological burden. Air pollution, destruction of the ozone layer, overwarming of

the earth's atmosphere, degradation and contamination of the soil, exploitation of nonrenewable and renewable natural resources, growing mountains of industrial wastes are the results of a pattern of industrialization and consumption that has until now mainly been geared to individual rationales of profit and utility and neglected considerations of national and global costs.

The main responsibility for the ecological burdens attributable to industry lies with the industries of the ICs. The overall burdens continue to accumulate, meanwhile not least due to the rapid growth of environmental degradation stemming from industrialization processes in the South. If the present patterns of industrialization and consumption in the North remained unchanged, the ecological collapse of the ecosystems in the North, the South, and at the global level would not be long in coming.

What is required if this is to be avoided is a swift transition to a concept of sustained development, in particular sustained industrial development (ecologically sustainable industrial development/ESID), i.e. patterns for present and future generations (UNIDO 1991, 15), without impairing basic ecological processes. These new patterns must in particular take into account:

–   eco-capacity: Use of nonrenewable resources at a rate guided by the availability of substitutes, use of renewable resources at a rate limited to their natural or managed regeneration rates, and the dispersion of industrial wastes at a rate limited to the assimilative capacities of ecosystems, thus preventing irreversible effects on basic life-support systems;

–   precaution: Adherence to the precautionary approach, which calls for environmental measures that prevent environmental degradation and attack its causes, thus anticipating threats of serious or irreversible damage;

–   anticipation: Development of procedures for accident prevention, thus reducing the risks of and potential losses associated with environmental emergencies;

- prevention: Prevention of pollution at its source in products and manufacturing processes rather than removing it after it has been created;

- efficiency: Minimization of resource consumption per unit of output and waste per unit of output, thus ensuring efficient use of man-made and natural capital;

- equity: Provision of opportunities for all countries to participate in the industrialization process, to benefit from the wealth generated by industrial activities and to apply the same principles of equity between genders and between present and future generations.

The transition from the dominant but unsustainable model of the North toward ESID challenges the entire industrial and commercial system. In the end, it will require conscious and deliberate changes in corporate goals, business practices, lifestyles, consumption patterns, and regulatory frameworks. ESID cannot be left to the market alone, since markets fail to internalize social and environmental costs. But neither can it be planned or driven solely by governments. Instead, both industry and governments need to become more open and accountable, and develop active partnerships with stakeholders, whether citizens, employees, or consumers. As the most recent developments demonstrate, there exist even today, both at the firm level and at the government level, considerable latitudes that come close to the concept of a sustained industrial development:

1. Technological latitudes for ESID: There exists considerable objective latitudes for substantially reducing environmental burdens via improved production processes and products if even today's "best practice technologies" are used. One interesting example is the development of the specific energy consumption of industry. For instance, industrial value added in Germany grew by over 80 % between 1970 and 1990. The energy requirements of industry fell in the same period by 20 %, even though energy prices, adjusted for inflation, are today lower than at the beginning of the 1980s. Nevertheless, the progress that has been achieved is as yet completely inadequate. What is crucial is not only to lower the specific energy consumption in production, but also to reduce the energy consumption associated with the use of consumer goods. Here, too, there are considerable technological latitudes (e.g. low consumption/low emission cars). It will, however, only be possible to ease substantially the burden on the environment when in industrial production the notion of closed cycles has gained currency and, in the use of industrial products by firms and consumers alike, the ecological dimension is taken into account.

2. ESID and emerging new technologies: The focus of enhancing the eco-friendliness of industrial production processes has thus far been on the so-called "end-of-pipe remedies". Meanwhile, however, a new trend appears to be emerging: the focus is shifting from the end-of-pipe remedies to a concept of "clean production", "i.e. a concept that addresses all phases of the production process or product life cycles with the objective of prevention and minimization of short-term and long-term environmental risks" (Robins and Trisoglio 1992, 159). Examples might include CFC-free refrigerators, low consumption/low emission cars, or the growing attention accorded to the notion of recycling as a design criterion for industrial products.

The fact that the number of firms about to redefine their business and technology strategies in the light of ecological requirements is on the rise is confirmed by numerous business polls recently conducted in Western industrial countries. Enterprises like Du Pont, one of the pioneers in the field of integrated environmental management, even believe "that an environmental management paradigm shift is under-way, so that, rather than regarding environmental quality as an added burden for business, it is now considered a vital part of a company's competitive advantage" (Robins and Trisoglio 1992, 168).

3. New regulatory frameworks: The changes of patterns of behavior of firms in industrial countries is essentially a response to tighter environmental regulations in the OECD. The time is foreseeable when the trend toward tightening environmental standards will intensify even further.

Countries like Japan (New Earth 21 Action Plan), Canada (Green Plan), and the Netherlands (National Environmental Policy Plan) have already formulated long-term action plans aimed at enforcing environmentally compatible modes of production. Early in 1993, the EC adopted a Community program for environmental policy and measures aimed at a sustainable ecologically compatible development and plans to draft a medium-term European plan, in line with the guidelines set out in Agenda 21, to encourage a new development model. The OECD has begun to prepare comprehensive environmental reports for individual member states.

In the DCs, too, there are signs of a distinct change in attitudes toward environmental and resource protection. The DCs continue to emphasize that environmental and resource protection must not be allowed to impair the latitudes open for economic growth processes. All the same, at the Earth Summit in Rio the DCs recognized that they too will in future have to accord high priority to environmental and resource protection within the framework of their national development strategies. Supported by the World Bank, 16 African countries have already begun to formulate national environmental action plans. A number of the young, dynamic ICs in Southeast and East Asia are about to review their development strategies and economic policies in the light of the requirements posed by sustainable development.

4. ESID and international competitiveness of ICs: The growing acceptance of the concept of environmental protection in the manufacturing industries of the industrialized Western countries could be due to the fact that environmental protection need not necessarily be especially expensive, even when no more than the technological opportunities available today are utilized. Thus, for instance, a recently published OECD study arrives at the conclusion: "Environmental compliance costs are not a large share of overall costs to industry: in most sectors, they constitute approximately 1 – 2 % of total costs or turnover ... This picture is not expected to change much even if environmental standards are tightened further in the pursuit of sustainable development..." (Stevens 1993, 22)

Environmental-protection measures will, to be sure, remain neutral in terms of competitiveness only if all countries participating in international trade are geared to similar environmental standards. It is for this reason that the running – but protracted – efforts directed toward establishing internationally binding environmental standards will prove essential to stepping up progress in the direction of sustainable industrial development.

National, regional, or international environmental standards as a rule reflect merely a minimum social or international consensus. Any orientation of business strategies in terms of those minimum standards will, however, in the coming years without doubt prove insufficient to remain competitive at the national and international level. The reason for this is that in all industrial sectors there are currently highly capable firms that have begun to use the eco-friendliness of their products as an important competitive factor. This new competitive factor will, in the view of the OECD study, gain in importance in the future, since "firms and sectors which invest early in environmental technologies can realize advantages in efficiency and productivity and put themselves in a position of a comparative advantage in meeting future regulations. Many firms in the OECD countries are starting to profit from the technical and marketing advantages of earlier investments in 'going green'" (Stevens 1993, 23). Seen this way, the future winners in national and international competition will tend to be the firms and countries which assume an offensive attitude toward environmental protection, and not those that go on the defensive (Weizsäcker 1994).

5. ESID and international competitiveness of DCs: DCs have thus far benefited in two ways from the change of the Industrialization pattern initiated in the OECD:

–   by pulling environmentally harmful industries out of the OECD,

–   by avoiding environmental-policy regulations, which has led to competitive advantages in a number of sectors (e.g. base industries, textile industries).

The phase in which it was possible to gain competitive advantages by avoiding or failing to internalize external costs will, however, soon be over. Marketing chances in OECD markets will in future be enjoyed only be those who offer products that comply with the standards of the OECD countries (Scholz et al. 1994). In the future, DCs will therefore also have to adhere to the concept of "clean production"; the OECD countries will no longer permit any eco-dumping, and consumers will come less and less to accept products that harm the environment or are based on environmentally questionable production processes.

ESID thus poses an enormous challenge to the DCs. They must adapt not merely to the radical technological progress triggered by new key technologies, but at the same time to the as yet relatively new challenges associated with the concept of "clean production". It must be assumed that, aside from the ICs in East and Southeast Asia, very few DCs will be in a position to come to grips, more or less on their own, with these new challenges. What is demanded of the ICs will be accordingly high, i.e. to support the DCs in their transition to ESID or to "clean production".

Footnotes

1   The present study is based on a policy paper prepared in 1993 for UNIDO.

2   Since modes of production, forms of regulation, social institutions, and individuals' needs and values are in the midst of a process of change, this study speaks not of a rough technological pattern or a rough technological-economic pattern but of a technological-organizational-social paradigm.

3   On the theory of viable systems, see especially Beer (1984); on the problems associated with the guidance and control of highly complex systems, see e.g. Willke (1983); see also Probst (1987), Chapters 5 and 6.

4   Brazil is a case in point. The production costs of soybeans are lower than in the U.S. (190 compared to 222 US-$ per metric ton). However, the price fob is higher due to inefficient means of transport (257 compared to 239 US-$ per metric ton). Furthermore, the final price increases because of inefficient harbor facilities as the ports in Rio de Janeiro and Santos are, respectively, 2.8 times and 5 times more expensive than the Rotterdam port.

Bibliography

Amsden, A. H., J. Kochanowicz, and L. Taylor (1994), *The Market Meets Its Match: Restructuring the Economies of Eastern Europe*, Boston (forthcoming)

Arndt, H. W. (1988), "'Market Failure' and Underdevelopment", *World Development*, Vol. 16, No. 2

Aubert, J. E. (1992), "What Evolution for Science and Technology Policies?", *OECD Observer*, No. 174

Audretsch, D. B., and H. Yamawaki (1991), *Sub-Optimal Scale Plants and Compensating Factor Differentials in U.S. and Japanese Manufacturing*, Berlin: Wissenschaftszentrum, FS IV 91-21

Balassa, B. (1977), *A 'Stages' Approach to Comparative Advantage*, Washington, D.C.

Barber, B. (1984), *Strong Democracy. Participatory Politics for a New Age*, Berkeley

Beer, S. (1984), "The Viable System Model. Its Provenance, Development, Methodology and Pathology", *Journal of Operations Research*, Vol. 35, No. 1

Bergsten, C. F. (1992), "The Primacy of Economics", *Foreign Policy*, No. 87

Bisang, R., and B. Kosacoff (1993), *Exportaciones industriales en una economica en transformacion: las sorpresas del caso argentino (1974-1990)*, Buenos Aires: CEPAL

Bitar, S. (1988), "Neo-Conservatism versus Neo-Structuralism", *CEPAL Review*, No. 34

Brainard, R. (1993), "Gobalisation and Corporate Nationality", *STI Review*, No. 13

Brocon, L. R., et al. (1991), *Saving the Planet*, New York

Brunner, H.-P. (1993), *The Recreation of Entrepreneurship in Eastern Europe: Neither Magic nor Mirage*, Berlin: Wissenschaftszentrum

Buitelaar, R., L. Mertens, and H. U. Schulz (1992), "The Challenge of Competitiveness. Manufacturing Enterprises and the Opening Economies of Latin America and the Caribbean", *Background Paper commissioned by the Inter-American Investment Corporation* (mimeo)

Chenery, H. B. (1975), "The Structuralist Approach to Development Policy", *American Economic Review*, Vol. 85, No. 2

Deutsch, K. W., et al. (1964), *The Integration of Political Communities*, Philadelphia

Dosi, G. (1984), *Technical Change and Industrial Transformation. The Theory and an Application to the Semiconductor Industry*, London

Dosi, G., K. Pavitt, and L. Soete (1990), *The Economics of Technical Change and International Trade*, New York

Esser, K. (1980), *Portugal. Unterentwickelte Metropole - entwickelte Peripherie?*, Kassel

— (1991), *Development of a Competitive Strategy: A Challenge to the Countries of Latin America in the 1990s*, Berlin: German Development Institute

— (1992), "Von der Binnenorientierung zur Weltmarktspezialisierung", in: A. Gleich et al. (eds), *Lateinamerika Jahrbuch 1992*

— (1993), "Latin America - industrialization without vision", in: idem et al. (1993)

— (1994), *Lateinamerika - Wettbewerbsorientierung und Integrationsdynamik*, Berlin: German Development Institute

Esser, K., W. Hillebrand, E. Kürzinger-Wiemann, D. Messner, and J. Meyer-Stamer (1992), *América Latina - Hacia una estrategia competitiva*, Berlin: German Development Institute

Esser, K., W. Hillebrand, D. Messner, and J. Meyer-Stamer (1993), *International Competitiveness in Latin America and East Asia*, London: F. Cass, GDI Bookseries, No. 1

Felix, D. (1994), *The Tobin Tax Proposal - Background, Issues and Prospects*, Berlin

Ffrench-Davis, R. (1988), "An Outline of a Neo-Structuralist Approach", *CEPAL Review*, No. 34

Fisher, P.A. (1992), "The Interface Between Manufacturing Executives and Wall Street Visitors - Why Security Analysts Ask Some of the Questions That They Do", in: J.A. Heim and W.D. Compton (eds), *Manufacturing Systems. Foundations of World-Class Practice*, Washington

Freeman, C. (1987), *Technology Policy and Economic Performance. Lessons from Japan*, London, New York

Fröbel, F., J. Heinrichs, and O. Kreye (1977), *Die neue internationale Arbeitsteilung*, Reinbek

Granovetter, M. (1983), "The Strength of Weak Ties", in: R. Collins (ed.), *Sociological Theory*, San Francisco

Habermas, J. (1992), *Faktizität und Geltung*, Frankfurt a.M.

Hammer, M. (1990), "Reengineering Work: Don't Automate, Obliterate", *Harvard Business Review*, Vol. 68, No. 4

Hayek, F.A. v. (1968), *Der Wettbewerb als Entdeckungsverfahren*, Kiel

— (1972), *Die Theorie komplexer Phänomene*, Tübingen

Hillebrand, W. (1991), *Industrielle und technologische Anschlußstrategien in teilindustrialisierten Ländern. Bewertung der allokationstheoretischen Kontroverse und Schlußfolgerungen aus der Fallstudie Republik Korea*, Berlin: German Development Institute

— (1995), *Shaping Competitive Advantages. Conceptual Framework and the Korean Approach*, London: F. Cass, GDI Bookseries, No. 6

Hillebrand, W. et al. (1992), *Technological Modernization in Small and Medium Industries in Korea With Special Emphasis on the Role of International Enterprise Cooperation*, Berlin: German Development Institute

Hillebrand, W., D. Messner, and J. Meyer-Stamer (1994), *Strengthening Technological Capability in Developing Countries - Lessons from German Technical Cooperation*, Berlin: German Development Institute

Hilpert, H.G. (1993), "Japanische Industriepolitik - Grundlage, Träger, Mechanismen", *Ifo Schnelldienst*, Vol. 46, No. 17-18

Hollingsworth, J.R., and W. Streeck (1994), "Countries and Sectors. Concluding Remarks on Performance, Convergence, and Competitiveness", in: J.R. Hollingsworth, P.C. Schmitter, and W. Streeck (eds), *Governing Capitalist Economies. Performance & Control of Economic Sectors*, New York, Oxford

Jaffee, S. (1993), *Exporting High-Value Food Commodities. Success Stories from Developing Countries*, Washington: World Bank, Discussion Papers, 198

Jonas, H. (1993), *Philosophie. Rückschau und Vorschau am Ende des Jahrhunderts*, Frankfurt a.M.

Jürgens, U., and W. Krumbein (eds.) (1991), *Industriepolitische Strategien*, Berlin

Jürgens, U., and F. Naschold (1994), "Arbeits- und industriepolitische Entwicklungsengpässe der deutschen Industrie in den neunziger Jahren", in: W. Zapf and M. Dierkes (eds), *Institutionenvergleich und Institutionendynamik. WZB-Jahrbuch 1994*, Berlin

Kaplinsky, R. (1988), "Industrial restructuring in LDCs: the role of information technology", *Paper preprared for Conference of Technology Policy in the Americas*, 1-3 December

Katz, J. (1993), "Organización industrial, competitividad international y política pública", in: B. Kosacoff et al. (eds), *El desafío de la competitividad. La industria argentina en transformación*, Buenos Aires

Keesing, D.B., and A. Singer (1992), "Why Official Export Promotion Fails. A survey of experience and interviews with experts", *Finance & Development*, No. 1

Klitgaard, R. (1991), *Adjusting to Reality. Beyond "State versus Market" in Economic Development*, San Francisco

Kochen, M., and K.W. Deutsch (1980), *Decentralization - Sketches Toward a Rational Theory*, Cambridge

Krumbein, W. (1991), "Industriepolitik: Die Chance einer Integration von Wirtschafts- und Gesellschaftspolitik", in: Jürgens and Krumbein (1991)

Levine, L., et al. (1991), *Energy Efficiency, Developing Nations and Eastern Europe*, Washington, D.C.

Lipsey, R. G., and W. Dobson (eds) (1987), *Shaping Comparative Advantage*, Toronto

Lundvall, B.-Å. (1988), "Innovation as an interactive process: from user-producer interaction to the national system of innovation", in: G. Dosi et al. (eds), *Technical Change and Economic Theory*

Marin, B., and R. Mayntz (eds) (1991), *Policy Networks*, Frankfurt a. M.

Mármora, L., and D. Messner (1992), *Jenseits von Etatismus und Neoliberalismus. Zur aktuellen Steuerungsdiskussion am Beispiel Argentinien und Südkorea*, Hamburg

Mayntz, R. (1991), *Modernization and the Logic of Interorganizational Networks*, Cologne: Max-Planck-Institut für Gesellschaftsforschung

Messner, D. (1990), *Uruguay: El sector industrial ante la apertura externa*, Berlin: German Development Institute

— (1993), *Stärkung technologischer Kompetenz in Bolivien*, Berlin: German Development Institute

— (1993a), "Búsqueda de competitividad en la industria maderera chilena", *Revista de la CEPAL*, No. 49

— (1995), *Die Netzwerkgesellschaft. Wirtschaftliche Entwicklung und internationale Wettbewerbsfähigkeit als Probleme gesellschaftlicher Steuerung*, Cologne (forthcoming)

Messner, D., and J. Meyer-Stamer (1994), "Systemic Competitiveness: Lessons from Latin America and Beyond - Perspectives for Eastern Europe", *The European Journal of Development Research*, Vol. 6, No. 1

Meyer-Stamer, J. (1992), "The End of Brazil's Informatics Policy", *Science and Public Policy*, Vol. 19, No. 2

— (1994), "Quem é realmente subdesenvolvido? Experiências com novos conceitos de organização industrial em países em desenvolvimento acelerado", *ILDESFESBRASIL*, No. 4

— (1995), *Governance in the Post-Import Substitution Era: Perspectives for New Approaches to Create Systemic Competitiveness in Brazil*, Brighton: IDS Discussion Paper, No. 349

— (1995a), "Micro-Level Innovations and Competitiveness", *World Development*, Vol. 23, No. 1

Meyer-Stamer, J. et al. (1991), *Comprehensive Modernization on the Shop Floor: A Case Study on the Brazilian Machinery Industry*, Berlin: German Development Institute

Michalski, W. (1985), "Leitlinien für eine Politik der positiven Strukturanpassung", *Beihefte der Konjunkturpolitik*, No. 31

Naschold, F. (1992), *Den Wandel organisieren*, Berlin

Nelson, R. (ed.) (1993), *National Innovation Systems: A Comparative Study*, Oxford etc.

OECD (1979), *The Case for Positive Adjustment Policies*, Paris

— (1988), *The Newly Industrializing Countries, Challange and Opportunities for OECD Industries*, Paris

— (1992), *Technology and the Economy: The Key Relationships*, Paris

— (1993), *Industrial Policy in OECD Countries. Annual Review 1993*, Paris

— (1994), *Science and Technology Policy Outlook: Part III - Selected Issues*, Paris (DSTI/STP(93)19/REV 1)

Oman, Ch. (1992), *Trends in Global FDI and Latin America, Inter-American Development Bank/OECD Development Centre, International Forum on Latin American Perspectives, Mobilising International Investment for Latin America*, Paris

OTA (1991), *Competing Economies. America, Europe, and the Pacific Rim*, Washington, D.C.: Congress of the United States, Office of Technology Assessment

Page, J. (1992), "The Magnificent Eight - World Bank seeks lessons from East Asia", *Far Eastern Economic Review*, 22.07.

Perez, C. (1985), "Microelectronics, long waves and world structural change: new perspectives for developing countries", *World Development*, Vol. 13, No. 3

Perez, C., and L. Soete (1988), "Catching up in technology: entry barriers and windows of opportunity", in: G. Dosi et al. (eds), *Technical Change and Economic Theory*, London and New York

Porter, M.E. (1990), *The Competitive Advantage of Nations*, New York

Powell, W.W. (1990), "Neither Market nor Hierarchy: Network Forms of Organization", *Research in Organizational Behaviour*, Vol. 12

Probst, G.J.B. (1987), *Selbstorganisation. Ordnungsprozesse in sozialen Systemen*, Berlin

Robins, N., and A. Trisoglio (1992), "Restructuring Industry for Sustainable Development", in: J. Holmberg (ed.), *Policies for a Small Planet*, London

Rosenberg, N. (1982), *Inside the Black Box: Technology and Economics*, Cambridge

Sabel, C.F. (1993), "Constitutional Ordering in Historical Context", in: F.W. Scharpf (ed.), *Games in hierarchies and networks*, Frankfurt a.M.

Schäfer, L. (1993), *Das Bacon-Projekt. Von der Erkenntnis, Nutzung und Schonung der Natur*, Frankfurt a.M.

Scharpf, F.W. (1992), "Wege aus der Sackgasse. Europa: Zentralisierung und Dezentralisierung", *WZB-Mitteilungen*, No. 56

— (1993), "Coordination in Hierarchies and Networks", in: idem. (ed.), *Games in Hierarchies and Networks*, Frankfurt a.M.

Schmalholz, H., & Penzkofer, H. (1993), "Innovationsstandort Deutschland: Ergebnisse des ifo Innovationstests", *Ifo Schnelldienst*, Vol. 46, No. 13

Scholz, I. et al. (1994), *Ökologische Produktanforderungen und Wettbewerbsfähigkeit: Neue Herausforderungen für chilenische Exporte*, Berlin: German Development Institute

Stevens, C. (1993), "Do Environmental Policies Affect Competitiveness?", *OECD Observer*, No. 183

Teitel, S. (1987), "Towards An Understanding of Technical Change in Semi-Industrialized Countries", in: J.M. Katz (ed.), *Technology Generation in Latin American Manufacturing Industries*, Basingstoke, London

Tobin, J. (1978), "A Proposal for International Monetary Reform", *Eastern Economic Journal*, No. 4

UNCTC (1990), *New Approaches to Best-Practice Manufacturing: The Role of Transnational Corporations and Implications for Developing Countries*, New York (mimeo)

UNIDO (1991), *Proceedings of the Conference on Ecologically Sustainable Industrial Development*, Copenhagen

Walzer, M. (1992), *Zivile Gesellschaft und amerikanische Demokratie*, Berlin

Weizsäcker, E. U. v. (ed.) (1994), *Umweltstandort Deutschland. Argumente gegen die ökologische Phantasielosigkeit*, Basel

Willke, H. (1983), *Entzauberung des Staates. Überlegungen zu einer Sozietalen Steuerungstheorie*, Königsstein

Womack, J.P., D.T. Jones, and D. Roos (1990), *The Machine that Changed the World*, New York

World Bank (1993), *The East Asian Miracle. Economic Growth and Public Policy*, Oxford etc.